The Hidden Meaning of Dreams

CRAIG HAMILTON-PARKER

Illustrated by Steinar Lund & Lynne Milton

STERLING PUBLISHING CO. INC.
NEW YORK

*This book
is dedicated to my father,
who recently passed to spirit,
and to my spiritual father,
Sathya Sai Baba,
who appeared to me in a dream
and changed my life.*

Library of Congress Cataloging-in-Publication Data

Hamilton-Parker, Craig.
  The hidden meaning of dreams / Craig Hamilton-Parker ; illustrated by Steinar
  Lund and Lynne Milton
    p.   cm.
  Includes index.
  ISBN 0-8069-7773-6
  1. Dream interpretation vs. Dictionaries. 2. Symbolism (Psychology) vs.
  Dictionaires. I.
Title.
BF175.5.D74H35   1999
                    154.6'3'03—dc21   99-20768
                                            CIP

            1   3   5   7   9   10   8   6   4   2

                    Designer: Chris Swirnoff

              Published by Sterling Publishing Company, Inc.
              387 Park Avenue South, New York, N.Y. 10016
                    ©1999 by Craig Hamilton-Parker
                 Distributed in Canada by Sterling Publishing
            % Canadian Manda Group, One Atlantic Avenue, Suite 105
                    Toronto, Ontario, Canada M6K 3E7
              Distributed in Great Britain and Europe by Cassell PLC
             Wellington House, 125 Strand, London WC2R 0BB, England
             Distributed in Australia by Capricorn Link (Australia) Pty Ltd.
        P.O. Box 6651, Baulkham Hills, Business Centre, NSW 2153, Australia

Contents

Introduction

Life is a dream, realize it

SATHYA SAI BABA

WHY DO WE DREAM?

Nobody knows for certain why we dream. One of the first people to come close to a scientific explanation was the Greek philosopher Aristotle. At first, he spoke of the soul exercising special clairvoyant powers, in accord with its divine nature, when freed in sleep from the body's constraint. However, he was to conclude that the function of sleep and dreams was to dissipate the vapors that rose from the stomach after food. Similarly, for many centuries it was believed that blood rose to the brain and caused congestion there. Sleep enabled the blood to drain back into the rest of the body.

Early 20th-century scientific theories about sleep and dreams proposed that lactic acid, carbon dioxide, and cholesterol collected in the brain during waking hours and were dissipated during sleep. In short, sleep and dreams were thought to be a function of elimination.

Today some psychologists are reconsidering these ideas. Although Aristotle and others were clearly wrong scientifically, they may have been correct that dreams are a physiological process. Some current theories propose that dreams are the body's way of "rebooting" the brain. Dreams dispose of memories that would otherwise clutter the mind with unnecessary remembered experiences. In particular they enable the emotions to become balanced. Dreams get rid of "garbage" and allow the brain's complex chemistry to stabilize. According to this viewpoint, without dreams we would simply overheat.

One of the biggest breakthroughs in dream experimentation came in 1952 when a researcher noticed that the eyes of sleeping subjects moved beneath their closed eyelids. In 1955, Eugene Aserinsky and Nathan Kleitman published a paper on these strange eye movements. They named them "rapid eye movements" and called this phase of sleep REM periods. REM sleep (also now know as paradoxical sleep) occupies 20 percent of an average night's sleep and alternates with orthodox sleep about every 90 minutes.

It has been found that during REM sleep the flow of blood to the brain increases, as does the brain's temperature, and both the penis in men and clitoris in women become erect. But most important, the brain shows a radical change in activity that can be measured on an electroencephalograph (EEG). A person awakened at this time usually remembers his dreams vividly. This discovery enables scientists to tell how often people dream; waking a subject during REM sleep guarantees the researcher a dream to study.

Most of us dream every 90 minutes, and the longest dreams—lasting 30 to 45 minutes—occur in the morning. Studies have shown that half of us wake during REM sleep and recall our dreams. The rest wake during non-REM sleep and are less likely to recall a dream. This may account for why many people believe that they never dream. The truth is, we all dream every night but most of us forget we were dreaming.

REMEMBERING DREAMS

Before you can work with your dreams, you need to learn how to remember them. A simple technique is to set the alarm clock a little earlier than usual. This may interrupt a period of REM sleep and you are more likely to recall a dream. Some authorities claim that many people unconsciously wake themselves at a time when they are not dreaming, because they want to repress what their dreams are revealing. It has also been shown that you are more likely to remember dreams if you are keen to have them. Reading this book will increase the likelihood that you will have more dreams—or so it may seem. In reality, you will only begin becoming aware of the rich dream life you already have, the difference being that you will be learning to take notice of your dreams and remember them.

Another technique is to drink a large glass of water before going to bed. You're likely to wake up during the night, which may interrupt a REM period and you may thereby recall a dream. I've tried the method and it works, but it's uncomfortable, and I invariably awaken to find that I've been dreaming of trying to find a toilet!

If you enjoy the whole process of dreaming and take pleasure in catching a dream before it fades into obscurity, then you are much more likely to improve your dream-recall skills. The best method is to write down your dreams. In Dream Experiment 1, you can read detailed instructions on how to keep a dream diary. I strongly advise that you do this. In time, you will treasure your dream diary and realize that the inner events it logs are as important as the story of your waking hours. Your dream diary is a permanent record of your spiritual development, reveals your hidden potential, offers solutions to problems, and gives insights that enable you to become a better person.

Some people prefer to tape their dreams. Apart from the expense of buying cassettes, this method denies you the opportunity to refer to past dreams quickly and compare similarities when making an interpretation. Talking about your dreams to someone else, however, will greatly help your recall. As you describe your dream, you are likely to remember snippets you had completely forgotten. Also, sharing dreams with a friend may help you with your interpretation of the dream's symbolism.

Talk to yourself about your dreams. Before going to sleep, say: "Tonight I will recall a dream." This will program your mind to remember and is an effective and proven method to trigger dream recall. In the morning, your first thoughts are likely to be about your dream. As with most dream techniques, perseverance brings success. If you still have difficulty remembering any dreams, try the following method, which was devised by Dr. Fritz Perls, the father of Gestalt therapy. Imagine that your dream is a person sitting in a chair opposite you. Ask this invisible dream person, "Why can't I remember you?" Next, listen to your own inner

voice. What is it telling you? This same technique can be used to help understand the meaning of a dream. Again, imagine that the dream is a person sitting in a chair opposite you. This time, cross-examine it about its meaning.

For many years, before becoming a Spiritualist medium and author, I was an artist. Art can be a wonderfully pleasurable way to work with dream recall. Simple sketches and doodles are best. Scribble a picture of something glimpsed from your dream and soon you'll be frantically trying to get down all the other dream images that flood your mind. Make a separate dream sketchbook or include your material in your dream diary. Surrealist painters such as Salvador Dali, Max Ernst, and René Magritte were masters at painting dreams but so were some psychologists. The Swiss psychologist Carl Jung painted some beautiful pictures of images from his dreams in a book he made. It was reminiscent of a Celto-Saxon illuminated manuscript. His "Red Book" included his dream guide, Philemon—a mysterious representation of the tree of life—and some beautifully executed mandalas. (See Dream Experiment 1 for details of how to create a dream diary)

If you still find that you cannot remember your dreams, do not become overly anxious. The more desperately we try to grasp the details of a dream, the more it eludes us. Instead, take your time waking up in the morning. Allow yourself to float between sleep and waking for a few moments and contemplate the dreams you remember. Think about them for a while before recording them. Start by writing just a few notes. These can trigger a more detailed recall later.

I sometimes make a simple "mind map" of keywords associated with the dream. These are circled and linked together. For example, suppose I dream of a station. I write down the word "station," draw a circle around it, and draw lines to other key words such as where the train was going, whom I saw, what the atmosphere was like, etc. Next I go back to each individual symbol and expand it, i.e., the man I saw in the station, what he was like, whether he reminded me of anyone, what he was wearing, etc. In this way, I quickly capture details without worrying about the chaotic plot that dreams follow.

Choose whatever method suits you best, but once you begin making a conscious effort to recall your dreams it will become easier every time.

TO USE THIS DREAM BOOK

There are many theories about the role and meaning of dreams, but most agree that they are the link between your conscious mind and your unconscious. In other words, they are messages from yourself to yourself. Dreams are an important key to self-knowledge. They can help you develop a more positive attitude and bring about greater self-awareness and self-healing. They can be used to solve your most difficult problems and may even tell you about the future.

If you use the methods described above to capture a dream, you're soon going to want to decipher its meaning. At first, this may appear difficult because you're confronted with what appears to be a load of nonsense. But it's not. Your thoughts, ideas, worries, hopes, and fears are all represented by symbols, metaphors, and images within your dreams. This is the language of dreams. The sleeping brain draws from your experiences and makes them into a mini play. A problem you have now may be compared to an event from your childhood, or a dream may be influenced by a movie you watched before going to bed. Sometimes, worries and anxieties that you've avoided for years return in dreams, asking to be resolved.

Psychology has many useful theories that can help you understand what your dreams are trying to tell you about your emotional state, ambitions, fears, and so on. When you look up a dream symbol in this book, you are first presented with a section explaining the meaning from a psychological perspective. This can help you decide what your dream says about your state of mind or hidden hopes and fears. This section often gives alternate meanings and considers the teachings of various schools and theories of psychology.

The second part of each entry deals with the mystical meaning of the dream. Included are references to ancient myths and to superstitions and mystical traditions from many parts of the globe. You may want to smile at the strange superstitions associated with some dreams, but this section also gives a taste of fascinating ancient dream traditions from around the world. I have also included my own psychic tips to help you use dreams to tell the future. You may also enjoy and be inspired by

the wise quotes at the end of some of the entries. I hope these will help you increase your positive attitude.

Furthermore, you will find dream experiments to try. These are based partly on psychology and partly on mystical tradition. Dreams are an exciting new area of self-discovery for most people. Once you start to work with dreams in a serious way you may discover that they are a means to greater spiritual awareness and lasting happiness. The experiments will demonstrate some of the remarkable psychological and spiritual power that dreams can unlock.

Finally, read the dream casebook and the dreams of famous people. Artists, musicians, generals, inventors, writers, scientists, sportsmen, and even politicians have all claimed that dreams have helped them to better themselves. Dreams can help you too.

COMMON DREAMS

Every dream can be interpreted in many different ways. No matter what psychologists and mystics say, the final analysis is up to you. I suggest that after reading this introduction you thumb through the A–Z section until you come to one of the dreams marked "Common Dream."

There are no limits to the mind's ability to generate an infinite abundance of dreams, but among this mass of imagery are a few common dreams that happen to almost everybody. Have you ever dreamed of falling, being chased, or losing your teeth? Most people have. Dreams like this are part of shared human experience, reminding us perhaps that there is only one race—the human race.

Dreams we have in common are, say some psychologists, humanity's spiritual heritage and connect us through myth and symbolism to the thoughts and feelings of our primitive ancestors. They recur throughout history and in all societies. Someone from a tribal society in Brazil or Africa may dream of being stalked by a wild animal; a person from London, Los Angeles, or Tokyo might express the same sentiments by being shadowed by a mugger. The core issue of the dream—the fear of being attacked—is the same.

You may recognize one of your own dreams in the "Common Dream" sections. If you've had one of these dreams, think about it for a while before you look up the meaning. Try also to recall the problems you were facing at that time. What sort of worries did you have? Were you concerned about money, love, self-esteem, or something else?

Now look up the meaning and see how much of the interpretation applied to you at the time. At the end of each "Common Dream" entry are a series of simple questions that you may want to ask yourself about the dream. Learning to ask the right questions about your dream is half the battle. You may want to apply some of the same questions to other dreams that you have. My interpretations may be wide of the mark when applied to your own dream. But it's your interpretation that counts the most. Treat this book as a useful guide, but trust your gut feeling. One of the most important lessons dreams teach is to listen to your intuition.

Here are a few additional questions you can ask about your dream:

1. *Who are the people in the dream?* In most cases, the people you meet in dreams represent aspects of yourself. Consider what aspects of your own personality they represent. Some dreams are also about your relationships with actual people from real life. Strangers may represent aspects of yourself you are unaware of. Similarly, animals may represent aspects of your instinctive nature.

2. *What is the mood of the dream?* The overall mood of the dream is important because this represents how you feel about the problem that the dream is drawing to your attention. In addition, the weather, the season, and the temperature can all represent your emotional state of mind.

3. *What symbols does the dream contain?* You can of course look up the symbols in this book, but remember to consider personal associations you have with the items you encounter in your dreams. Gestalt psychology insists that your dreams are about you and you alone. See every part of your dream as a part of yourself or some aspect of your personality. Remember that many symbols are unique to you.

4. What does the setting say about me? The dream environment you find yourself in may represent the way you feel about yourself or your situation.

5. *Does this dream remind me of another one?* Dreams often run in sequences, so you may already have worked out the meaning of some symbols. If you keep a dream diary over many years, you will be intrigued to note that some dreams take up a theme from dreams you had years earlier.

THE PSYCHOLOGICAL MEANING OF DREAMS

There are many psychological theories about dreams, but by far the most important pioneers of modern dream interpretation are the Austrian psychiatrist Sigmund Freud (1856 - 1939) and his Swiss colleague, Carl Gustav Jung (1857 - 1961). You will find many references throughout the text to these two important figures.

Freud believed that the mind consisted of three aspects, which he called the ego, the super-ego, and the id. The unconscious side, the id, Freud believed consisted of instinctive drives. As the instincts always aimed at pleasure, Freud called the id the "pleasure principle." Most desires expressed in dreams, he believed, were sexual.

The super-ego was the name Freud gave to what he called "the moral principle." This corresponded roughly to the "conscience," which he believed had a social origin. Freud lived in a sexually restricted age, so it was natural for him to conclude that the super-ego (conscience) would be in continual conflict with the id (instinctive sexual desires). The super-ego lived in a state of constant tension, trying to control the irrational sexual demands of the id. Between these two opposites sat the conscious self, acting as a referee between the rival claims of these two unconscious forces. Freud called this the "reality principle" and named it the ego. According to Freud, everyone is to some degree neurotic because the ego will never be able to satisfy the demands of both the id and the super-ego.

Freud believed that in sleep the ego relaxed and could no longer adjudicate between the conflicting forces of the id and super-ego—that in sleep the super-ego stood guard over the ego, protecting it from the overwhelming instinctive urges of the id. Freud believed that dreams were a symbolic language by which the id tried to communicate with the ego, but its messages were censored by the super-ego. The result was that the messages from the unconscious come to the ego only in a disguised or misrepresented way.

Carl Jung was originally a follower of Freud but fell out with him because Freud was intransigent in his belief that sexuality was the defining factor of the psyche. He refused to refine or change his views in the light of compelling evidence, and he became arrogant and inflexible.

At first, Jung accepted much of what Freud taught, but in time discarded the concept that the unconscious was a repository for rejected emotions and desires. He believed that the unconscious offered ways to inner wholeness and healing and contained whatever we needed to resolve our psychological troubles. He further believed that dreams gave access to these positive energies. He saw the human condition not as a continual conflict between super-ego and id but as a striving toward the wholeness of the self. Instead of believing that they masked hidden desires, Jung believed that dream symbols expressed what was happening in the unconscious and made an impression on the dreamer.

≈≈≈

Jung also proposed the theory of the collective unconscious, a part of the mind containing information common to all human beings. This could explain why in widely different cultures dreams with specific symbols have the same meaning. For example, many myths, fairy tales, and rituals around the world are almost identical but originated independently. Jung believed that these were expressions of archaic symbols that emerged spontaneously from the collective unconscious and he named these symbols archetypes.

Many of Jung's ideas are presented in the body of this book.

THE MYSTICAL MEANING OF DREAMS

Early human cultures believed that dreams were glimpses of the divine world, possibly messages from the gods or supernatural beings. We will never know for certain what prehistoric people thought of their dreams, but some cave paintings are reminiscent of the strange world of dreams.

It is certain that the earliest cultures considered dreams to be of great importance and treated them with the utmost reverence. For example, the ancient Egyptians believed that the gods communicated through dreams. The ancient priests devised spells to bring dreams forth. Egyptian dream books have been discovered—as have spells—to call upon the god Besa, who would answer questions through dreams.

One of the earliest written records of dreams and their meanings is a papyrus of circa 1250 B.C. It records 200 dreams and their interpretations according to the falcon-headed god Horus. A better-known example is found in the biblical book of Genesis, in which the Pharaoh's precognitive dream of seven fat cows is correctly interpreted by Joseph as prophesying seven years of plenty and seven years of famine for ancient Egypt.

The ancient Greeks also believed that dreams were messages from the gods, although this was disputed by Aristotle in *Parva naturalia*, in which he argued that dreams were fragments of recollections of events of the day. However, the general belief throughout the ancient world was that dreams were the gods' predictions of the future.

The oldest surviving comprehensive book of dreams and their meanings was compiled by Artemidorus of Ephesus in the second century A.D. It was translated into English in the seventeenth century and was reprinted 32 times before 1800. Freud used it in his research. It influenced many of the first dream dictionaries. This and the other dream dictionaries that followed were primarily concerned with predicting the future through dreams—an art known as oneiromancy.

The mystical meanings in this book include traditional interpretations of dreams, many of which originate from these ancient sources. They also include many superstitions associated with dreams that I discovered in my research of folklore archives of cultures around the world.

Whether old superstitions can help you see the future is questionable, but a great deal of empirical evidence suggests that dreams can be prophetic. Your dream diary will help you identify prophetic dreams, but the most interesting glimpses of the future can come through a phenomenon called Lucid Dreams.

LUCID DREAMS

Most of the time we do not realize that we have been dreaming until we have awakened. However, certain dreams are so vivid, they fall into a category of their own. Mr. George P., of Kansas, U.S.A., wrote to my Internet column, saying: "I was dreaming that I was directing a new film of the classic movie *Rebecca*. Suddenly the characters, the set, the landscape all seemed to burst into life. Everything became amazingly vivid. It was then that I realized, 'I'm dreaming.' The film *Rebecca*, as you may know, has a tragic ending, but now I recognized that I was the director and could make the movie end any way I pleased.

"As the 'film' progressed, I understood that the dream was my way of sorting out my uncertainties over a new relationship in my life with a girl named Becky," continued George. "I realized that I was behaving badly and woke up with a resolve to completely change my attitude."

George became conscious that he was dreaming while the dream was in progress. In other words, he "woke up" in the dream. His ordinary dream became incredibly vivid and George discovered that he could not only change the content of the dream but was also consciously resolving his feelings at a very deep level.

The Dutchman van Eeden called these dreams "lucid dreams" and recognized that they were not only extraordinarily vivid but could be controlled. It has been reported that 73 percent of the population have had at least one lucid dream, and lucid dreaming comes naturally to between 5 and 10 percent of people.

Lucid dreams have been described for centuries but are only recently being taken seriously by modern-day dream researchers. Freud and Jung, although aware of them, virtually ignored them in their theories. Yet references to them are found in the writings of Aristotle. Saint Augustine recorded a lucid dream of his friend Gennadius, and Saint Thomas Aquinas also reported them.

One of the first systematic studies of lucid dreams was made by the ancient yogis of Tibet, who are well known for their extraordinary psychic, physical, and mental abilities. According to esteemed Oxford scholar Evans-Wentz, Tibetan adepts mastered the lucid dream state. "The yogi learns by actual experience, resulting from psychic experimentation, that the character of any dream can be changed or transformed by willing that it shall be."

Tibetan adepts mastered the lucid dream state, using lucid dreaming as a means of realizing that the senses are illusory and that the only reality is Nirvana. "The Universal Creation, with its many mansions of existence, from the lowest to the highest Buddha paradise, and every phenomenal thing therein...are but the content of the Supreme Dream."

A fascinating discovery of the Tibetans is that lucid dreams can be used to trigger extrasensory perception and as a means of traveling outside the body.

See Dream Experiment 2 for information about how to trigger a lucid dream.

THE MYSTICAL GOAL DREAMS

Sleep and dreams are necessary for every living being. Without them we cannot live. Sleep is one of life's most joyful experiences; it restores our energy and brings us peace. The Hindus believe that during sleep we breathe in living energy called prana. During sleep, the *prana* life force becomes like a holy fire that awakens the spirit and energizes us.

According to the Vedas (the holy texts of the Hindus), during sleep the true spiritual seeker may be able to "reach the Brahma-loka which the person has earned by his Karma." In other words, during sleep it is possible to merge with the Supreme Consciousness—something yogis seek through years of meditation.

According to the Vedas, during the sleep state the *jivi* (the ego) is capable of experiencing the whole of reality. It can perceive the outer world, the inner world, and other dimensions. In addition, it can see into previous lives and into the fabric of time.

In dreamless sleep, the *jivi* can enter the region known as the Brahma-loka, the divine plane of existence that transcends all physical worlds. This is the supreme bliss of exalted consciousness. This state can be realized effortlessly during sleep. But the Hindu sutras and teachings note that the experience is temporary, not lasting. To the realized person, dreams can bring bliss and liberation from attachment, deep sleep can rejuvenate the life energy, and dreamless sleep can give a taste of the ultimate reality. Dreams reveal reality. What was once hidden can now become manifest

Dream Experiments

Keeping a Dream Diary

*I never travel without my diary.
One should always have something
sensational to read in the train.*

OSCAR WILDE

If you're serious about using dreams to unlock your psychological and spiritual power, you're going to need plenty of material to work with. We know from EEG (electroencephalographic) readings that sleep follows approximately 90-minute cycles. We dream an average of four to five times a night, with the most vivid dreams occurring just before awakening. Everybody dreams every night, but not everyone is in the habit of remembering dreams.

Merely wanting to remember your dreams can help improve your recall dramatically. Another simple and effective method is to keep a dream diary.

1. Invest in a good-quality hardcover blank book that will last you some years. Your dreams are an important part of your life and in years to come you may want to refer back to dreams you have now. A cheap notebook is likely to get lost or be forgotten about.

2. Resolve to enter at least one dream into your book every night for a month. This will establish the habit of remembering your dreams. At first, it will take an effort, but soon the half-remembered fragments will become long, intriguing epics.

3. Draw a line down the middle of each page. In the left column, write your dream; and in the right, your interpretation.

4. Keep your dream diary beside your bed at night. As you go to sleep, reach out and touch it. Say, "Tonight, I will remember a dream." By doing this, you are issuing a command to your unconscious, and it will obey you. Once you've programmed this biological computer, relax as you normally would and go to sleep. Your unconscious will do its job automatically.

5. In the morning, write your dream in the left-hand column. If you cannot immediately recall a dream, write whatever is on your mind. This will help you remember your dream. Always make sure to write something, even if it is only a few sentences.

6. If you remember a dream, write it down. Don't worry about spelling, grammar, or the sequence of events. Get the dream on paper before it fades. First write down things you heard, because auditory information is the most easily forgotten. Make notes about your feelings and reactions as well as the people, places, and events in the dream. If possible, indicate colors and even the weather conditions; these can say a great deal about your state of mind.

7. Now, in the right-hand column, write down what you believe the dream is saying about you. Write down what you think the people, places, and events symbolize about you and your life.

8. Next, look up the symbols in this book and see if my interpretations shed light on the dream's hidden meaning. Remember, there are no hard and fast rules. The symbolism of every dream is unique.

9. Finally, at the top of the page give the dream a title and date.

Lucid Dreaming

(see also Introduction)

*If you can dream and not make
dreams your master...*

RUDYARD KIPLING

 f you've been keeping a dream diary, already your dreams have started to become more vivid. The decision to dream increases the probability that you will remember your dreams. Again, a little preparation before you go to sleep will increase the likelihood that you will have a "lucid dream."

Research indicates that most lucid dreams occur in the morning between five and eight o'clock. Dream laboratories encourage lucid dreams by stimulating sleepers with mild electric shocks, flashing lights, or noise. As most of us don't have gadgetry available, we need to rely on our own dream-catching ability and pre-sleep planning.

1. During your normal daytime activities stop and ask yourself: "Is this a dream?" Of course it's not, but by establishing the habit of questioning you will soon ask yourself the same question when you're asleep.

2. Repeat the same question before you go to sleep. Again you are encouraging your unconscious to question reality. By doing this regularly, you will realize that you are dreaming and "wake up" in the dream.

3. It may take some weeks of persistence, but once the questioning procedure is established, you will trigger a lucid dream. To reinforce the technique, tell yourself before retiring: "Tonight I *will* have a lucid dream." I've found that it's best to actually say this out loud six or seven times and then silently while drifting off to sleep. This helps program the unconscious, making you aware of a dream as it is taking place. You'll soon have a lucid dream.

4. As soon as you realize you have "awakened" in a dream, try to increase your awareness without waking up. For example, when you become aware that you are dreaming, try to look at your hands. By doing this, you are taking control of the dream. If you see your hands, bring them together. Again, by controlling your actions in the dream, you are preparing to control the dream itself. During a lucid dream, if you sense that you may fall back again into ordinary dreaming, look at your hands again. This will help you maintain your alertness and control within the dream state.

5. Lucid dreams can help you sort out fears and phobias. For example, if you regularly dream of being chased, in a lucid dream you can turn the tables on the attacker and take control of your fears. You can also give yourself an ego-boost by dreaming of being in an extremely successful and glamorous job or of being the sexiest person on earth! You will carry this subliminal self-confidence into your waking life and alter your behavior patterns.

6. Lucid dreams can also be used to see the future. Once you take control of your dream, try influencing it to see ahead in time. Imagine that you are looking into a crystal ball or traveling in a time machine. These dream techniques can trigger your latent clairvoyance and give you genuine insight.

Problem Solving

*To all, to each, a fair good-night,
And pleasing dreams, and slumbers light!*

SIR WALTER SCOTT

 n the days of ancient Greece, people believed that while they slept they could receive messages from the gods. A person who wanted a message would sleep in a sacred area or temple and by the morning would be given a dream to resolve the problem or to be shown the future. In particular, this widespread oracular technique evolved into the healing cult of Asclepius at Epidaurus, which became a center of pilgrimage from all Greece.

But you don't have to sleep out under the stars or entombed in a mysterious temple for this technique to work. Your sleeping brain is the biological computer that can answer problems for you while you're safely tucked in bed. Program it to work for you using dream incubation—a simple technique to make your dreams solve problems.

1. Before you go to bed, decide what problem you would like your dream to solve for you. It might be about a relationship, work, money, or sex—the choice is endless. Now, write down the problem in the form of a question. Just before going to sleep, put the piece of paper the question is written on under your pillow. You have just downloaded the software for your inner computer.

2. As you fall asleep, run the question through your mind. Try to turn it into picture form. For example, if it's a relationship that needs sorting out, imagine the two of you laughing and chatting together. Keep the imagery happy—avoid negative thoughts.

3. Now put the issue out of your mind, and let your dream do the rest. Look forward to your dream. Treat it like a letter that you look forward to receiving from a friend.

4. If you tell yourself that you're going to dream, you probably will. When you awaken, write down a detailed account of your dream. What does the dream say about the specific question you asked? Of course, the dream will give its answer in a symbolic way. Interpret the images as directly relating to your question.

Dreaming of Past Lives

The jivi (ego) experiences all that is seen, heard, and contacted by the mind in the outer world, as well as the impact of all that it could not see, hear, or contact by the mind. Besides these, the jivi might construct experience in dreams and witness such experiences undergone during previous lives.

SATHYA SAI BABA (SUTRA VAHINI)

ave you ever dreamed about your childhood and clearly remembered events that you could never have managed in a waking state? Things that are almost impossible to recall flash into your mind as if they happened only moments ago.

Some authorities claim that every event that has ever happened to us in life can be recalled by the human memory. Hypnotists have discovered that subjects can recall long-forgotten events with incredible accuracy. For example, the page of a book glimpsed for a few seconds in childhood can be recalled word for word by an adult and repeated verbatim.

Mystics and psychics believe that dreams not only reveal the memories of this life but all our past incarnations as well—human and animal!

Here are some tips to help you to uncover your past:

1. Go through your dream diary and note all your recurring dreams. Many of course will be about problems and anxieties that have taken you years to resolve or accept. However, some of them may be memories from past lives that are trying to get your attention.

2. Dreams of past lives often have a "grand dream" quality. Note all the dreams that have this feeling.

3. Recurring dreams not filled with anxiety may hold clues to past-life events. Why do we have

such dreams? Anxiety-producing recurring dreams occur because of unresolved inner conflicts, but pleasant recurring dreams seem to serve no psychological purpose. Unpleasant dreams may also be memories from past lives, but it's much easier to work with pleasant experiences to help our recall. It's easier to remember something supportive rather than horrors we've forced out of our normal awareness.

4. Yogis say that memories of past lives come spontaneously to the spiritually advanced adept. Our past lives have pretty much of an equal measure of good and bad—though probably some more good than bad to have given us the opportunity to reincarnate in a human form.

5. As you build a picture of your past lives from the clues and fragments scattered throughout your dreams, more information will be revealed to you. What you focus your attention on grows in strength. Dreams are the doorway to discovering who you once were.

ᗞreams of the ᖴuture

And one day there will come a great awakening when we shall realize that life itself was a great dream.

CHANG-TZU (C. 350 B.C.)

ince the earliest times, people have believed that dreams can foretell the future. Many techniques can enhance this natural ability of the unconscious, but one of the most effective is hypnagogic dreaming. This extremely vivid form of dreaming is most often experienced upon first dropping off to sleep. To a large extent, it is under the control of the will. Hypnagogic images are often described as possessing an overwhelming sense of reality, with much detail and supersaturated color.

If you've ever been bombarded by a storm of incredible images as you fall asleep, with exceptionally bright colors and vivid images, you've probably wondered how your mind can conjure up such amazing scenes. The pictures are strange, surreal, even frightening. They rise and fall in a kaleidoscope of color and form. They stream in and out like the most complex computer animation. It is a truly fascinating experience.

Sigmund Freud and Belgian psychologist J. Varendonck together proposed that these dreams are pre-conscious thought and wishful thinking. Others claim that these dreams possess a physiological basis related to the onset of sleep or partial awakening. The truth is, no theory adequately explains why these overwhelmingly real images are generated by the mind.

Other psychics and I have found that some of the images generated by this state of consciousness are glimpses of future events:

1. Choose a target event in the future to dream about by cutting out a current news story and placing it beside your bed.

2. As you get sleepy, hold the clipping in your hands. Allow yourself to completely relax, and watch your body and mind. (See Experiment Six on daydreaming for detailed relaxation methods.)

3. As you drop off to sleep, notice the images flashing before your mind's eye. The trick is to hold yourself on the brink between being awake and asleep. Do not let yourself fall asleep. Your brain will generate many images. Observe them with the eye of an artist. Look at the form, color, texture, and detail. Try to hold each image for a few seconds before letting it go and letting another arise. The more you concentrate, the more intense they will become.

4. By now the power of your imagination will be so enhanced, it will be easy to visualize a television in front of you.

5. Hold the image. Now imagine that you are switching the channels until you come to a news channel. Now let the hypnagogic images dance on the TV screen. Think "News." Now think about your clipping. Do images appear on the screen that relate to your clipping?

6. Now here's the difficult part: pull yourself

back to normal consciousness. Hypnagogic dreams are so relaxing, this will take real effort and dedication. Next, scribble down as many images as you can remember into your dream diary. You'll have to be quick, because the images fade very, very quickly.

7. Look up your notes in the weeks to come to see how many of the images were correct predictions. My wife Jane and I were once employed every week on one of the U.K.'s top TV shows to predict "Next Week's News" today. This dream technique proved extremely accurate, and we were able to predict events with an uncanny accuracy.

DREAM EXPERIMENT 6

Waking Dreams

In Xanadu did Kubla Khan
A stately pleasure dome decree:
Where Alph, the sacred river, ran
Through caverns measureless to man
Down to a sunless sea.

SAMUEL TAYLOR COLERIDGE

he above passage from the wonderful poem "Kubla Khan" about the Mongol emperor was written while Coleridge daydreamed. He fell asleep and began composing the beautiful poetry without effort. Upon awakening he found he could slip in and out of the dream, enabling him to write down 54 lines of extraordinarily beautiful verse.

Unfortunately, someone knocked on the door and interrupted his revery. A "person on business from Porlock" kept Coleridge busy for over an hour. When he returned to his writing, the dream had gone. The remaining 255 lines that Coleridge had "heard" were lost forever.

As this example shows, daydreaming can be a very useful and creative activity. Charles Dickens wrote most of his best work after a period of light reverie. Mozart, Napoleon, Edison, and

Churchill were all known to catnap to solve problems or restore their energy. They all slept less than five hours a night. Try it for yourself:

1. Set aside 15 minutes every day to recharge yourself. You could perhaps forgo a cup of coffee and use one of your breaks at work for this purpose. It would be circumspect to tell your colleagues what you are doing beforehand so that you're not interrupted. When they see how efficient you've become, they may want to nod off with you!

2. Sit comfortably with your eyes closed. (This in itself increases the beneficial and restorative alpha brain waves.)

3. Notice how your breathing slows down as you become increasingly relaxed. Let all tension fall away. Concentrate on your feet. Feel them relax. Work upward, and be aware how perfectly at peace every one of your muscles becomes. You may notice how relaxed your shoulders feel and how your tension eases, particularly around your eyes. Become the observer of your body.

4. Now become the observer of your mind. Notice how it has become more peaceful as your breath and body relax. Watch your thoughts. Observe them, note them, but do not follow them. For these few moments, let go of all thought. Be the watcher.

5. Don't be tempted to get sucked into the thinking process. Soon images will arise in your mind's eye. In a relaxed manner pay attention to them. Observe every detail but do not follow the thoughts. Notice that one picture leads to another and another and another....Let the images flow. Stay awake but let go of thought. You are daydreaming.

6. Observe the images and pictures for the duration of your designated break.

7. When you start to work again, you will not only feel greatly refreshed but also your thinking will be remarkably clear. Solutions to problems you have been working on will suddenly become apparent. Your unconscious was working while you were relaxing, and ideas will pop into your head effortlessly.

Dream Dictionary

ABANDONMENT (SEE ALSO REJECTION)

Psychological Meaning This dream may express your unconcious feelings of being foresaken. Do you feel that people neglect you emotionally? Do you harbor feelings of resentment, such as an unresolved problem from childhood? The dream may be saying that you need to express your feelings and that you need to be understood by others. On another level, it may be pointing out that you need guidance with some life issue. For example, perhaps you hope for an authority figure to help you take control of your life. Many people have dreams of abandonment after the death of a loved one. Grief brings a strange mixture of emotions: anger, resentment, depression, panic, and abandonment. These feelings are all part of the healing process.

Mystical Meaning Abandoning something unpleasant indicates good financial news ahead. But the omens are bad if you abandon something or someone you cherish—destiny sees troubled times. However, if you are the one abandoned, reconciliation will happen quickly.

ABBEY

Psychological Meaning A spiritual aspect of your life is about to unfold. Buildings in dreams usually represent the dreamer, the body, or the various levels of the mind. The abbey is a holy place, ancient and free of pomp. It symbolizes the true you—your spiritual self. If the abbey is very old, consider exploring ancient wisdom, such as stories of the Celts or early Christian myths. These dreamlike tales will help trigger your spiritual awakening as you draw upon the ancient memories within the unconscious.

Mystical Meaning Generally considered a good omen but, according to superstition, a young woman dreaming of entering an abbey foretells an illness. A ruined abbey predicts that plans will fail, and if your way to the abbey is blocked, it augers that you will be saved from a ruinous mistake. To dream of an abbot means an illness or plot is afoot, but an abbess denotes happy friendships.

ABDOMEN (LOWER BODY)

Psychological Meaning The dream may have a physiological cause, such as constipation or indigestion. Emotionally something may be worrying you, something you "cannot stomach," something you want to get out of your system. Possible sexual innuendo; in a woman it may indicate a desire for motherhood.

Mystical Meaning Traditional folklore says that dreaming of your own abdomen promises great things that you must work hard for. It can also foretell of infidelity. A shriveled abdomen warns of lies; a swollen one promises ultimate success; and blood warns of tragedy within the family.

ABYSS

Psychological Meaning Real or imagined problems may be creating anxiety. You may feel you are "falling into a pit of despair" or feel that your situation is abysmal. You may be "standing on the brink" of something and fear "taking the plunge." These feelings threaten you now, so it is important to examine your situation and discover the cause of these unpleasant emotions. A dark abyss may symbolize the unknown part of yourself. If you feel anxious, perhaps you are uncertain what you will discover about yourself and about your hidden feelings and fears. Dreams of this nature sometimes occur when you are thinking about death—not as a prediction but as a way of reminding yourself of the importance of life.

Mystical Meaning An abyss is considered an omen foretelling financial difficulties. Be extremely careful in your business dealings. Some archaic systems warn of romantic, employment, or health problems ahead. The collective advice is: proceed with great caution in all your affairs.

ACCIDENTS

I keep dreaming of car crashes. Do you think my dream is forecasting the future? I am beginning to fear driving.—A.G., California

Psychological Meaning Your dream is not necessarily a premonition of the future. Nightmares of this type reveal deep anxieties and fears. The car crash may symbolize your emotional state. Are you driving yourself too hard? Perhaps you should slow down a bit. If your life feels as if it's set for disaster, examine your mistakes and resolve to set a new and better course. If the accident happens to someone else in your dream, examine your heart. Do you feel suppressed hostility toward that person? Unexpressed jealousy, resentment, or hatred may be finding its release through your dream. Or perhaps the dream refers to accidents of a different kind, such as saying the wrong thing or accidentally forgetting your anniversary.

ASK YOURSELF

1. *Do I feel emotionally at peace with myself?* Probably not, but use the dream as a prelude to a more peaceful you. Get yourself in balance. Relax, listen to music, and take up yoga, meditation, or some other therapeutic activity. And stop punishing yourself!

2. *Have I had similar dreams before?* If yes, try to recall your emotional state at the time. Remember the lessons you learned in the past and apply them again to today's circumstances.

Mystical Meaning The soothsayers says to take care for 24 hours following the dream. Some dream traditions believe that accidents at sea pertain to love affairs but accidents on land symbolize business problems

———

ADULTERY

Psychological Meaning Don't take these dreams too literally; they usually highlight inner fears. Perhaps you are worried about your sexuality or you desire something not in your best interest. The dream is a way your unconscious expresses its sexual urges. Sometimes it does this in ways that go against what is socially acceptable or advisable.

Mystical Meaning A legal action may befall you if a man dreams of adultery. A woman dreamer will lose the affections of her husband. (Ancient dream dictionaries, written before the advent of women's rights, predicted far worse consequences for women than for men who had this dream.)

AGE (SEE ALSO CHILD)

Psychological Meaning The dream may highlight concerns about getting older. Try not to be dated with your opinions and be a little younger at heart. However, an old man or woman in a dream may be symbolic of superior wisdom within you. Listen to the advice and guidance your higher self brings you. If you dream of being a child, you may be drawing upon the psychological resources that are the foundation of your personality.

Mystical Meaning To dream of old people brings good luck, but to dream of growing old yourself is a sign of failure. To see a friend grow old suddenly is a warning of disappointment from that friend.

AIR (SEE ALSO ELEMENTS AND WIND)

Psychological Meaning Air represents wisdom and clarity. As an element it symbolizes spiritual concerns but in a dream it may be a

---

FAMOUS DREAMER

J. W. Dunne
Author

J. W. Dunne, in his book An Experiment with Time *(Macmillan 1927), said he dreamed he was on an island on which a volcano was about to erupt. He explained that he tried to warn the French authorities about the impending explosion and that 4,000 lives were in danger. On waking, he immediately made an entry into his meticulously detailed dream diary. A few days later Dunne opened his newspaper to read of the eruption of Mount Pelée on the French island of Martinique. An estimated total of 40,000 lives had been lost. (See also Time)* warning of the dangers of losing contact with reality. As a breeze or wind it may represent the spirit that inspires or the life force that animates.

Mystical Meaning Old dream books claim that to dream of air means your hopes will wither away.

AIRPLANE (SEE ALSO FLYING)

Psychological Meaning To dream of being in an airplane may show you "rising above" your troubles. An airplane is a symbol of transcendence and release from psychological or material difficulties. The sky is a symbol of the expanded consciousness of the higher self. Your airplane dream expresses your desire for greater awareness or spiritual knowledge. An **airport** or air journey may indicate a new departure in your life. This could include a new job, new relationship, or an adventure. To a Freudian psychologist an airplane is a phallic symbol by virtue of its forceful, penetrative motion. You may have high ambitions and want to progress in life swiftly to achieve your goals as quickly and directly as possible. Airplanes are the quickest way to get to a destination. Alternatively, you may simply desire to travel or have a vacation. A dream of a plane crash can show that you are overly ambitious and have set your sights too high. Materially or emotionally, you may be expecting too much and you may have doubts about your ability to reach your goals.

Mystical Meaning Most modern superstitions say that dreaming of an airplane indicates that money is on the way. If you are the pilot, you will succeed in a business adventure. If the plane crashes, a business will fail. Gypsies say that dreaming of an airplane indicates that you must share your enterprises with your relatives.

ALCHEMY

Psychological Meaning Carl Jung believed that the secret art of the alchemists was a system of symbols used to bring about the transformation of the personality from its base state (lead) to exalted spiritual consciousness (gold). Alchemical symbols are archetypal images from the unconscious. If you dream of alchemy you may be experiencing a period of inner transformation. It may be painful but is most definitely for the best.

Mystical Meaning Alchemy was the medieval equivalent of modern psychology. Its strange symbolism can still invoke unconscious forces that bring about positive inner transformation.

ALIEN (SEE ALSO FOREIGNER AND UFO)

Psychological Meaning Assuming that you weren't abducted during the night, dreaming of an alien indicates an encounter with an unfamiliar part of your psyche. You may feel that this unfamiliar part of yourself is hostile or an enemy. Your first step should be to find out what it is and get to know this neglected aspect of yourself. For example, you may be behaving in ways that are "alien" to you or have feelings that are "unlike you." It is unhealthy to repress or neglect these components of your nature. What at first appears frightening because of its unfamiliarity may in time become a mentor and ally. Your alter ego may have something good to offer you. Also, the alien may represent a situation you have recently experienced. When you start a new job you may at first feel alienated or like an outsider. Alternatively, you may feel that emotionally you are in another world from everyone else.

Mystical Meaning Aliens are (arguably) a product of modern times, so no traditional folkloric interpretations exist.

ALTAR

Psychological Meaning From a religious standpoint, an altar can have a number of meanings. It is a place of sacrifice, so the dream may symbolize a personal sacrifice you have made or intend to make. Or it may mean that you have sacrificed something within yourself; something within you must die if a new, happy life is to be born. For example, you may sacrifice the ego so that more sincere feelings can manifest in your life. In addition, the altar may symbolize the wedding of the unconscious and the conscious mind—the union of opposites compensates for the development of a one-sided personality. Or it may symbolize the consecration of something you deem sacred. Many dreams express themselves with puns. Maybe the dream is suggesting that you should "alter" your plans.

Mystical Meaning To dream you are inside a church is usually considered a bad omen. It warns of error and repentance. To see a priest at the altar warns of quarrels and problems at home or in business. However to see a church from the outside brings good fortune and blessing.

ANCHOR

Psychological Meaning You may be looking for greater security, as an anchor represents a stabilizing force. It may also symbolize an influence in your life that brings greater steadfastness and strength. For a career person, it can show a desire to be the "anchorman" (or woman). Alternatively, the anchor may represent something negative that is holding you back and restraining your freedom. For example, you may feel shackled to a relationship that isn't working or feel tied to an emotional problem. A Freudian interpretation of the dream might be that you are chained to your mother and dependent on her. (The sea can symbolize the mother.)

Mystical Meaning An old superstition states that if a woman dreams of an anchor, one of her children will choose a life as a sailor. It is also favorable for a sailor to dream of an anchor. For the rest of us, it means a change of residence or foreign travel. Generally it is considered a good omen, but if the anchor is in the water or partly hidden in any way, expect disappointment.

ANGEL (SEE ALSO FLYING)

Psychological Meaning As a practicing medium I believe that the spirit world can contact people through dreams, and that angels are the higher spirit beings that help humanity progress spiritually. Since earliest times, angels have been known as messengers from God. In a psychological sense, this could be a message from parts of yourself leading to greater fulfillment and happiness. Wings suggest flight and transcendence. If the angel is sinister, recognize it as something in your life that may cause trouble. Pay attention to these things and give them expression in your life. Dreaming of the Angel of Death is not necessarily an omen of death. It may symbolize your anxiety looking for a way to express itself.

Mystical Meaning Considered a fortunate dream symbol, to dream of angels predicts good fortune in love, partnerships, and friendships. Several angels means you will receive an inheritance and, if an angel enters your home, you will be wealthy.

ANGER

Psychological Meaning Dreams give the opportunity to express feelings and emotions sometimes impossible to express in waking life. You may have some aggression within yourself that you have not acknowledged fully. The dream may be suggesting that you become more assertive and stop taking a passive attitude toward your circumstances. Perhaps you feel undervalued, rejected, or jealous or you harbor hostile wishes toward someone close to you. Someone angry with you might represent a characteristic in yourself that you dislike. Are you angry with yourself? Do you feel guilty about an issue? Psychologist Alfred Adler believed that aggressive drives motivate most people but can be sublimated and directed into creative channels.

Mystical Meaning According to some timeworn sources, anger in a dream denotes an unlawful trial that awaits you. It foretells disappointment in love and attacks on your character. However, if you are angry with a stranger, unexpected good news is on its way. An invitation is likely.

ANIMA/ANIMUS (SEE ALSO HERO/HEROINE)

Psychological Meaning The *anima* is the feminine principle in the male psyche. It is often symbolized by a beautiful young woman. She may leave the dreamer determined that he must embark on a heroic quest to meet her again. The dreamer may mistakenly look for the "girl of his dreams" in the outside world, but in reality the dream points to the motivation to discover the feminine part of himself. Integration of both the masculine and feminine sides of your nature leads to psychological health and wholeness. Similarly, the *animus* is the masculine principle in the female psyche. A woman may dream of it in the guise of a beautiful young man or a hero figure.

The *anima* (the feminine principle in a man) can also take a negative role. Instead of providing spiritual inspiration and a more balanced view of

ANIMA/ANIMUS

life, it can appear in dreams as moody, irritable, and oversensitive. If the "woman of your dreams" is like this, it may signal that these destructive characteristics are dominating your personality.

Similarly, the *animus* (the masculine principle in a woman) can also be a destructive force. According to Jung, a negative *animus* causes a woman to be opinionated, argumentative, rigid, controlling, and excessively critical of herself and others. Jung believed that everyone should strive to find a proper balance between the positive qualities associated with both the *anima* and *animus* and integrate these into the personality.

Mystical Meaning   The wisdom of yore says that to dream of a young man or woman is a sign that there will be a reconciliation of family disagreements.

ANIMALS (*SEE ALSO* HORSE, LION, FISH, MONKEY, BIRD, *ETC.*)

Psychological Meaning: Animals signify primal, instinctive, and sometimes base desires. Your dream may be drawing attention to an aspect of your nature you undervalue or part of yourself you repress. Try to get in touch with the natural you. Be more spontaneous and less rational. Within everyone is a deep instinctive energy that has a transforming power. A dream of eating an animal is a classic mythical symbol that represents assimilating natural wisdom. Fighting an animal may show that you are grappling with your shadow—the hidden part of yourself that the conscious mind has rejected. Animals guarding a treasure can represent brutish passions preventing you from realizing your true spiritual potential. Animals may also express certain qualities: a dog may represent devotion, a cat may represent intuition, a tiger may represent fear, and a pig may symbolize gluttony and bad behavior. Animals can represent people (sly as a fox, slippery as a fish, strong as an ox, a lying snake, etc.).

Mystical Meaning   To dream of an animal is considered an omen for the future. Peaceful cows and bulls are considered particularly good omens, but try hard never to dream of crocodiles, dogs, or cats, for these bring troubles. In the Far East, to dream of a green monkey means that a medicine will not work. Indeed, to even think about a green monkey while taking a medicine stops it from working. Next time you take a medicine, try *not* thinking about a green monkey—it's impossible, of course!

ANXIETY

Psychological Meaning   Nobody knows for certain the function of sleep. Many scientists say that people sleep in order to dream—that dreams are the brain's way of bringing the emotions back into balance. Experiments have shown that people consistently deprived of dream sleep suffer from emotional disorders. Dreams resolve anxieties and restore psychological equilibrium. It's quite natural to have dreams that express anxieties and emotions that cannot be asserted in everyday life. Freud believed that anxiety dreams disguise repressed aggression or resentment. Where anxiety appears in dreams, look for repressed feelings or desires that initiate anxiety. Freud identified repressed childhood feelings of resentment, jealousy, and hostility toward parents and family as giving rise to these dreams.

Mystical Meaning   Superstition says that anxiety dreams have the opposite meaning, showing that a worry will very soon be relieved. In some ways this is true, for by expressing your fears in your dreams you come a little closer to resolving your hidden fears.

APE (*SEE ALSO* MONKEY *AND* SHADOW)

Psychological Meaning   The dream may simply be a pun: i.e., "You're making an ape of yourself." You may be making an egotistical mistake of some kind. Apes are known to be gentle, so the dream may also symbolize the part of you that wants to behave more naturally and return to a simpler archaic past. A sinister ape may symbolize the dark, repressed side of your nature.

Mystical Meaning   Bad news, I'm afraid. To dream of apes means that people will deceive you, and mischief is afoot. Be particularly careful of false promises connected with business. If the ape is in a tree, someone close to you will tell lies that cause widespread trouble.

ANIMALS

APPLE

Psychological Meaning The apple may be considered a sexual symbol. It is the forbidden fruit associated with the fall of Adam and Eve in the Garden of Eden and so with sin, by which sex is usually meant. Freud pointed out that eating is connected with sexuality, because the mouth is the first erogenous zone discovered by young children. From a Freudian viewpoint apples stand for lasciviousness. Your dream may be saying that you have a sexual appetite and want to taste the fruits of life. Alternatively, apples may symbolize knowledge, since this is what Adam and Eve gained after falling from innocence. On a mundane level you may have personal associations with the symbol, such as an Apple computer or the Big Apple, or it may be as a symbol of good diet and health.

Mystical Meaning It is a good omen to dream of apples, particularly if they are red. Dreaming of ripe and sweet apples promises you will be rewarded, but if the apples are sour you are in danger of loss because of your own foolishness. Fallen apples on the ground warn of false friends. And if the apple is decayed, all your efforts will be hopeless.

ARMOR

Psychological Meaning An armored, or shielded, individual is likely to protect himself from spontaneous emotional interaction with people. In dreams, these are protective symbols against anxiety. Ask yourself what it is you want to protect yourself from. Is it an inner fear? Is there something you need to defend yourself against? Examine the causes of this feeling and you may discover you need not be so guarded. With more self-confidence, openness, and social ease, you would not have to take such extreme measures to protect yourself from the outside world. The dream may also show that you are preparing to do battle. Armor may represent the fact that you are confident and well prepared.

Mystical Meaning If you dream of wearing armor, including breastplate, chain mail, or thick leather jerkin, tradition says you are taking life too seriously. Lighten up and enjoy life. People who believe in reincarnation may interpret this dream as a reference to a past life. If historical facts are revealed within the dream, see if they are true. You

may be recalling mysterious memories from lives long ago.

ARREST (SEE POLICE)

ARROW

Psychological Meaning A Freudian psychologist interprets this image as a male sexual symbol. Favored by Cupid, an arrow can represent the penis in its ability to penetrate. It has associations with male violence and aggression. (In the hymn "Jerusalem" William Blake refers to "my arrows of desire.") Arrows can also represent something that goes straight to the mark. The dream shows how to reach targets you have set for yourself. Perhaps you should focus on one specific goal and set about achieving it.

Mystical Meaning "Expect journeys, entertainment, and festivals," says one medieval source. To dream of being struck by an arrow means you have a secret enemy. A broken arrow portends disappointment in love or business.

ARTIST

Psychological Meaning This may represent the creative and intuitive side of your nature. You may feel a need to express yourself and may have the urge to be more creative. If you're painting a picture it may show the way you picture your situation at the moment. You are probably starting to see things more clearly.

Mystical Meaning You may have to revise your plans in order to attain recognition. If you talk about art in your dream you may expect an upturn in your business or professional status.

ASHES

Psychological Meaning After the fire has gone, dull, lifeless ash remains. You may be feeling that the good times are over and nothing of value is left in your life. Alternatively, you may be raking over the past or dwelling upon something that is finished. Ashes may represent a failed relationship or ruinous business enterprise. In Hinduism, ashes are a symbol of the indestructible soul. After everything has been reduced by fire, ash is what remains. It is the indestructible part of yourself.

Mystical Meaning To dream of ashes is a bad omen. Crops will fail, business deals will go wrong, and children will cause problems for their parents. Gypsies, however, say it means you will finally cease to mourn lost chances of the past. Many tribal societies consider ashes to be a positive symbol of fertility and good luck. In England and the United States ashes are said to ward off evil spirits.

AUDITION

Psychological Meaning Social vulnerabilities are highlighted, and you may fear that you are unable to communicate effectively with others. You feel as if your social role in life is being tested. Dreams like this may occur soon after starting a new job or undertaking a socially challenging role. You may also dream of being unable to make yourself heard over the noise of others, of being laughed at or tongue-tied, or you may have a feeling of impending disaster. All these images express feelings of social vulnerability. An unruly audience may show your inability to get your ideas across. The absence of an audience may show a lack of recognition.

Mystical Meaning Most dreams associated with actors, actresses, and the stage are considered fortunate, but to see them wandering and penniless foretells that your good fortune will be reversed. To dream of public speaking is also fortunate, but speaking from a pulpit bodes sickness and business failure.

AVALANCHE

Psychological Meaning You may fear a disaster or failure. Perhaps your intuition has identified a flaw in your plans that needs urgent attention. Carefully examine the other images in the dream and see if you can identify the cause of the fear or warning. The issue may be emotional. Are you "as cold as ice"? Your frozen feelings may be causing you problems. Loosen up or you may cause an avalanche of out-of-control emotions.

Mystical Meaning Mystics say it is tremendously fortunate to dream of an avalanche, particularly if you are buried in the snow! It portends profit and wealth. To see others buried in an avalanche indicates a change of surroundings.

AWAKENING (SEE ALSO LUCID DREAMS)

Psychological Meaning To dream of awakening may represent a new awareness that is unfolding in your life. However, it may mean that you are on the verge of lucid dreaming. In this remarkable state of consciousness you "wake up" in the dream and realize you are dreaming *as the dream is taking place*. In this state, the dreamer can direct the dream like a film director. Lucid dreams can be used creatively or to help resolve psychological problems. For example, someone with recurrent dreams of being chased, in a lucid dream might be able to turn around, stare down the stalker, and unmask the fears hitherto run from. Native Americans have practiced lucid dreaming techniques for centuries.

Mystical Meaning To dream that you are awake and walking though a beautiful landscape denotes good times ahead after a period of difficulty. People who consciously cultivate their psychic ability use special techniques to "wake up" during dreams in order to look into the future. One method is to imagine being in a time machine. The dream moves into the future and the psychic receives a premonition of future events.

AXE

Psychological Meaning This ominous symbol can be interpreted in a number of ways. Perhaps you are worried about your job, of being "given the axe." Or do you want to chop something out of your life? If you dream of an executioner's axe, you may be feeling guilty about something you have done. In this case, the axe may represent judgment and punishment. An axe used to chop wood may show that you need to divide your problem into more manageable parts. Chopping down a tree may symbolize removing the old so that the new can sprout fresh and may necessitate a change in lifestyle or circumstances.

Mystical Meaning Apart from clearly warning of danger, the axe has some strange dream lore associated with it. To dream of a shiny axe signifies gratifying rewards, but a dull one means loss of prestige. An axe also means that you will soon hear from friends. For an unmarried woman, this dream means she will meet the man of her dreams but he will never have a cent!

BABY

Psychological Meaning A baby may represent something new in your life. Does it cry for attention? Do you feel content with this new situation? A baby can also symbolize your own inner nature, pure and uncorrupted, or may say that you are innocent of an accusation. It could show the vulnerable part of you that needs protecting, or perhaps you are nurturing some new ideas or feelings. New Age gurus speak of loving the magical child within and advise expressing the innocent carefree side of yourself. Your dream may be telling you to follow this advice. To dream of a baby, of course, may show that your maternal instincts are seeking expression; you may simply wish for a child.

Mystical Meaning Surprisingly, most old dream books believe that dreams of babies have nothing to do with prophecies of pregnancy. For example, if a woman dreams she is nursing a baby, she will be deceived by someone she trusts.

BACK

Psychological Meaning The back of the body, the back of an object, stage, or building symbolizes parts of yourself hidden from view. The back may also represent secrets you keep from other people or aspects of your personality you would prefer not to think about. If the dream gives you a feeling of unease, these hidden traits may have negative connotations. You may have pushed away feelings of guilt, shame, fear, or self-disgust.

Mystical Meaning Traditionally, evil is said to stand behind us. The preacher may say "Get thee behind me, Satan." People who believe spilling salt brings bad luck throw some over their left shoulder and into the eye of the devil. Your dream may point to an aspect of your life that is now over, a situation you have "put behind you." Maybe your dream contains some other play on words: Is someone getting your back up? Do you feel you need a pat on the back?

BACKWARD

Psychological Meaning To dream of walking or moving backward means you are taking retrograde steps in your life. What you seek from life appears to be moving away from you. You may have a feeling of failure, an inability to achieve your goals and aspirations. Alternatively, the dream may be telling you that the best policy at the moment is to retreat. Why exhaust yourself in a fruitless struggle? Rest and gather your strength so that you can try again later with renewed vigor and self-confidence.

Mystical Meaning Some tribal societies believe that evil spirits can be thwarted by a dramatic change in routine. Walking backward is one way to confuse demons that bring bad luck. To dream of walking backward therefore indicates that better luck is on its way.

BAG

Psychological Meaning The bag represents psychological qualities you carry through life. For example, if the bag is full of junk, it may represent attitudes and worries you burden yourself with. In this case, your problems are of your own making—consider ways to unload your problems. Perhaps you can lighten your load by adopting a cheerful attitude. Similarly, the bag may represent responsibility. The dream may be suggesting that you share the burden you presently carry on your own. If the bag is filled with food or items of value, the dream may be showing that you are gathering ideas or new knowledge in your waking life.

Mystical Meaning Dream superstition says that dreams of paper bags forecast financial bad luck, cloth bags bring business success, and leather bags forecast unexpected journeys. The heavier the bag, the more success you'll have.

BAKING

Psychological Meaning This dream can represent plans you are nearly ready to put into action. You should soon benefit, for bread represents the qualities of nourishment and wholesomeness. This dream can also represent pregnancy. The oven is the womb and the bread is the growing child. But don't rush off to buy a crib and baby booties. The dream is most likely a metaphor rather than a prediction of an actual birth. It may be showing the development of a new idea or a period of spiritual development.

Mystical Meaning To dream of baking brings good luck, say the old superstitions. Unfortunately this dream prophesy only applies to men.

BABY

BALDNESS

Psychological Meaning If you dream of losing your hair you may be worried about your self-image and how others perceive you. You may feel insecure and anxious. You may also feel that you do not have the power to succeed in an undertaking and may be unconsciously reminded that Samson lost his strength when his hair was cut. You may also harbor fears of aging or loss of virility. If you are losing your hair in real life, this dream expresses your anxieties about it. Surrender some of your vanity and your stress level will decrease.

Mystical Meaning European and American cultures hold that to dream of being bald is a signal of financial loss. However, this belief is reversed in the Batoro tribe, whose people live between lakes Albert and Edward in East Africa. Fertility and prosperity are guaranteed the Batoro bride only if every hair on her head and body is shaved before she marries. The bride is then covered with copious quantities of oil. To dream of being bald is therefore an auspicious sign.

BALLOON

Psychological Meaning If the balloon flies freely in the sky, this dream may be expressing your desire for freedom or escape from an oppressive situation. You seek to rise above the conflicts of daily life. Festive balloons can also represent a celebration of some kind or a personal achievement. However, the dream can also have a negative connotation. Do you have an inflated opinion of yourself? Be careful, for a balloon full of wind can easily burst—and so can your ego.

Mystical Meaning Traditional interpretations say that to dream of traveling in a hot-air balloon warns of an unfortunate journey. Alternatively, it may indicate that you can see the way ahead. Look at the landscape. Does it represent the landscape and pathway of your future?

BANK

Psychological Meaning A bank, and particularly the vault, represents your inner storehouse of psychological potential. Your unconscious is telling you to start using your inner reserves of skill and energy. It's no good locking your talents away. The dream symbolism may be more literal than this. The dream may show your practical need for financial security. You are being shown that your circumstances are more secure financially than you fear. However, if you dream of robbing a bank, it may suggest that you are expending too much energy and are in danger of depleting you inner resources.

Mystical Meaning If you dream of putting money into the bank it means money is coming your way. If you dream that the coffers are empty, it forecasts financial doom.

BAPTISM

Psychological Meaning The baby or adult being baptized is you. The next stage of your life, your plans, and your hopes are all being blessed by your higher self. You are being reborn into something new and better. A baby being baptized may represent a new way of being, a new attitude toward life, or a new approach toward others. Immersion in water represents death, and emergence represents resurrection and new life. The old, negative, you has died, and it is likely that this new you will be successful. Your new attitude will bring positive things to you. The dream may also be spiritual. Your faith in God has been renewed and you are coming closer to self-realization and spiritual fulfillment.

Mystical Meaning If you dream of drinking water from a baptism, you will be a great and famous singer.

BAT

Psychological Meaning The early Christians considered bats birds of the devil because of their association with darkness and their similarity to rats. Bats share the sexual lust of the devil. (The devil is a corruption of the cloven-footed god Pan, who played his pipes in celebration of nature and sexuality.) In particular, vampire bats, which take human form in Bram Stoker's *Dracula*, represent predatory sexuality, for it is only virgins' blood that they can drink. Maurice Richardson, in *Psychoanalysis of Ghost Stories*, observes that Dracula, with his dark heroism and superhuman image, has an unconscious erotic appeal for women. He argues that the story only makes sense analyzed from a Freudian standpoint. Alternatively, a vampire bat may represent a person in your life who is depleting you of self-confidence or resources.

Mystical Meaning To dream of one of these universally loathed creatures is a portent of disaster. They are considered omens of injury or death. Because of their blindness, bats are also considered prophecies warning of danger to the eyes. Fortunately, superstition also has an antidote for these terrible dreams: Carry a bat bone in your pocket and you'll come to no harm. In parts of Europe people believe that a bat's right eye carried in a waistcoat pocket will make a person invisible.

BATH

Psychological Meaning Bathing represents psychological cleansing. You are trying to get rid of old attitudes. Water can symbolize your emotional nature. You may be trying to cleanse yourself of negativity. Perhaps you have feelings of guilt or are uncomfortable with your feelings. You may feel that your natural sexual feelings are dirty thoughts. It has also been suggested that a bath symbolizes the waters of the womb and represents a desire to escape back to the security of the amniotic waters.

Mystical Meaning It was once believed that the act of washing cleansed a person not only of the dirt from the body but also of the sins from the heart. But to dream of bathing is a mixed blessing, for in many countries it is believed to wash away your good luck.

BEARD

Psychological Meaning A beard symbolizes the wild and primitive man within you—your untamed sexual side. According to Freud, a man who dreams of having his beard cut fears castration; beard-cutting symbolizes loss of sexual confidence. If a woman dreams of growing a beard it may show her desire to play a man's role—to have a more powerful job or be more assertive. Long beards are associated with old age and wisdom. A wizened old man with a long, gray beard represents the insight that comes from the unconscious. It is your own higher self that can guide you to greater knowledge and understanding.

Mystical Meaning An Arab will not thank you if you pull his beard, for this is considered a terrible insult. Wars have been waged over lesser sins. Similarly, in Europe and America to dream of a beard signifies a fierce battle ahead.

BEREAVEMENT (*SEE* DEATH)

BIRD

Psychological Meaning Because of their ability to fly, birds universally represent spirituality. The sky is the unfettered realm of the spirit and, like the winged gods of old, birds show that some process within your psyche is bringing you wholeness, healing, and balance. Birds are the soul's desire for transcendence. They may also show your desire to escape from something you consider to be banal and commonplace. You may want to be free of a situation and have a desire to take wing. Or is it a habitual attachment or negative attitude you want to rise above? In mythology, birds are often messengers from the gods. In psychological terms it may show that the unconscious is offering you new insight and solutions to your problems. To dream of freeing a bird from captivity relates to releasing your own emotions or primal energies.

Birds can also symbolize aspects of relationships. Thieving birds, such as magpies, may suggest adultery or some other threat to a relationship. Territorial birds, such as blackbirds, can represent jealousy. According to Freud, birds are sexual symbols that represent the penis. Many people still call attractive young women birds. Finally, a flock of birds may represent your need to be one of a group that you admire and identify with.

Mystical Meaning For centuries it has been considered a good omen to dream of birds. Here are a few of the most common superstitions: albatross, good luck coming; buzzard, beware of gossip; cock, if it crows you will receive good news soon; dove, a peaceful solution to your problems will be found; eagle, business success; geese, improvements ahead; hawk, a bright future awaits you; magpie, a change of plan in matters of the heart; owl, beware of disappointment; stork, family problems are imminent; turkey, bad luck unless you dream of killing or eating it.

BIRTH

Psychological Meaning For a woman, dreams about birth may simply reflect your thoughts and feelings regarding motherhood. As a symbol, birth can represent the possibility of a new beginning or a period of personal growth. The same imagery is used in everyday language: "giving birth to a new idea," you may refer to a project as your baby. Sometimes bringing something new into your life can be a painful process.

For Jung, dreams about birth were important because they represented a stage in the individuation process. Put simply, this is the growth of the human psyche to maturation and wholeness. Birth therefore represents the start of an important new phase in your life and personal psychological development.

Mystical Meaning To dream of giving birth brings good luck to married people but trouble to single women.

BITE (SEE ALSO FOOD)

Psychological Meaning Young children sometimes bite in order to express aggressiveness. You may have unexpressed, perhaps childish, feelings of anger or resentment that need to be recognized and perhaps expressed. If you are the one being bitten, it may illustrate that you feel pestered by a problem or difficulty. If an animal bites you, consider what aspect of your instinctive nature it represents. The dream may also point to an outer problem. For example, being bitten by a shark may be a play on words telling you something like "be careful of that loan shark."

Mystical Meaning To dream of biting means you will suffer a loss because of an enemy—or so they say.

BLACK (SEE COLORS)

BLIND

Psychological Meaning If you dream of being blind, it may represent your refusal to see the truth. Perhaps you reject something about yourself or your situation. Do you feel you have lost your sense of direction in waking life? Or are you so bigoted in your opinions that you refuse to see any other point of view except your own? Perhaps your religious experiences are one of "blind faith" rather than tolerance and spiritual inquiry? Truth frees you from the painful bondage of ignorance. Open your eyes!

Mystical Meaning In mythology Wotan sacrificed an eye to get the runes. Similarly, the visionary Tiresias in ancient Greece was blind. Blindness as a mystical dream symbol represents swapping outer vision for inner vision. The dream may therefore represent wisdom and self-knowledge

BLOOD

Psychological Meaning Blood is a symbol of life. If you dream of losing blood, you may be suffering from exhaustion or may feel emotionally drained by a situation. Blood can also symbolize passion, especially love, anger, or even violence. Women sometimes dream of blood at the start of their menstruation.

Mystical Meaning In many ancient rituals, participants drank the blood of sacrificial animals. This represented sharing the power and strength of the gods. Similarly, to dream of drinking blood may be a grisly symbol for receiving new vitality.

BLUE (SEE COLORS)

BOAT

Psychological Meaning A boat may represent traveling through emotional times. In particular, water may be a symbol for the emotions. If the water is rough, you may be feeling emotionally fraught in waking life. If all is calm and still, you may feel that your emotional life at this time is "smooth sailing." To dream of missing the boat may show you've missed an opportunity.

Mystical Meaning In mythology, boats, such as the ferry across the river Styx, could represent the transition from this world to the next. As a symbol, it may represent the passing from one phase of life to another. You may be making a clean break with the past.

BOMB

Psychological Meaning The dream may be telling you something about a potentially explosive situation you have to deal with in your waking life. Alternatively, it could be something within yourself, such as a desire to explode with anger about an issue that's affecting you. Similarly, the bomb could represent repressed desires and drives that are likely to explode if not dealt with. Proceed with caution and exercise inner calm. Why not take up meditation? It will help defuse this inner time bomb.

Mystical Meaning A heated argument will have a happy ending if you dream of a bomb, says dream superstition.

BONDAGE

Psychological Meaning If you dream of being tied up it may indicate that aspects of your psychological life are too tightly controlled. You may be restricting your need for self-expression or feel that you are a prisoner of your circumstances. You may have hidden potential you refuse to acknowledge or you may be repressing your true feelings. Perhaps the dream shows that you are held captive by the banal and commonplace, that you have a need for the inner freedom that comes with spirituality. You may want to set yourself free. You may also fear that a forthcoming event, such as a marriage, new job, or the birth of a child, will curtail your freedom.

The dream may also show that you try to dominate others. Do you try to dominate or emotionally smother your kith and kin? Some people dominate others by placing them under an obligation; this secures dependency or indebtedness. Such a controlling attitude will never bring happiness.

Bondage of course also has erotic overtones. Freud believed that dreams of bondage were an allegory for repressed sexual fantasies. These, he said, dated back to childhood when our parents dominated us. Alternatively, it could symbolize your desire to be more sexually submissive or could illustrate that you have unacknowledged sexual passions.

Mystical Meaning To dream of being tied up means that, contrary to your better judgment, you will yield to love.

BONES (SEE ALSO SKULL)

Psychological Meaning Your dream may be showing you the "bare bones" of a situation. Being stripped or cut to the bone may signify a sudden insight or an attack on your personality. To dream of fractured limbs may represent a threat to the foundations of life, and to personal power. If you dream of broken bones, you may have discovered a fundamental weakness in your plans or psychology. Sometimes, bones refer to a skeleton in the closet.

Mystical Meaning Goddesses with strings of skulls around their necks or waists refer to the negative, devouring side of time. Perhaps you fear getting older?

BOOK

Psychological Meaning This can symbolize knowledge, wisdom, or the intellect. It may also say that you are more concerned with theory and opinion than with putting what you know into practice. A book may represent a record of the story of your life.

Mystical Meaning Shun evil in all its forms if you dream of old books, say the ancient sages of dream lore.

BOSS

Psychological Meaning Bossy dream characters were nicknamed "top dog" by Fritz Perls, founder of Gestalt therapy. They are similar to Freud's notion of the super-ego. These bullies scold and lecture other dream characters, who rapidly assume the role of what Perls called "underdog." These are aspects of your personality you are ashamed of and that you try hard to ignore. For a healthy psyche, it is important to accept all aspects of yourself and let all the inner parts of yourself come to expression. In your imagination, ask each dream character to speak to you. The answers they give may reveal a great deal about your hopes, desires, and fears.

Mystical Meaning The first dream books were of course written for the literate upper classes. And so they say that to dream of being bossed around is a sign of incompetence but to dream of being the master means you will rise to a high position in society.

BOTTLE

Psychological Meaning Are your emotions bottled up? The bottle in your dream may represent how you are pushing your feelings back inside rather than letting them express themselves in waking life. The contents of the bottle illustrate the nature of the emotions. Champagne may show your need to socialize; poison may represent evil thoughts; red wine may represent passions; and milk may show the need to nurture new ideas or feelings. If the bottle is empty, you may have exhausted your inner resources. You may be feeling drained and empty inside. Regularly recording your dreams may suggest ways to fill this inner vacuum.

Mystical Meaning In many myths the genie is kept locked in a bottle until released by the hero. In dreams, the genie may represent the powers of the psyche which at first appear dark and menacing because unconscious but are transformed when brought under conscious control. The story of Aladdin and his magic lamp was based on these very ancient myths.

BOX

Psychological Meaning By opening a box you reveal things that were once hidden. This dream may be a symbol of spiritual exploration—you are getting to know the contents of your psyche. If you find bad things in the box or opening it fills you with fear, you may be uncovering things about yourself or your environment that make you feel anxious.

Mystical Meaning In the Greek myth Pandora's box represents the negative aspect of woman. This beautiful temptress is the source of all evil, yet her name means "all-giving." As a psychological dream symbol this story illustrates a man's fear of the dark, feminine side of his own nature. It may also show the way the unconscious projects its own negative complexes and attitudes onto reality.

BREASTS

Psychological Meaning Most likely, this dream symbol is a sexual one that shows your desire for love. However, it may also represent a mother's nurturing qualities. You may be nurturing new ideas and plans. A Freudian interpretation would ask you to question whether you are too attached to your real mother—an attachment that may be preventing you from achieving your independence.

Mystical Meaning If a woman dreams of having shriveled breasts she will be disappointed in love; if they are buxom and lily white, she will be rich. The ancient books say nothing about men who have these dreams.

BRIDE/BRIDEGROOM (*SEE ALSO* MARRIAGE AND ANIMA/ANIMUS)

Psychological Meaning A bride may represent the peak of feminine force within us. For a man she is an anima figure, the feminine side of his nature. Similarly, a bridegroom may represent the masculine, animus, side of a woman's personali-

ty. The most psychologically healthy people are those who integrate both sides of their nature.

Mystical Meaning Most fairy tales use the same symbolism found in dreams. Many end with "They got married and lived happily ever after." This typical happy ending is a classic dream symbol for the union of the masculine and feminine forces within the psyche.

BRIDGE

Psychological Meaning A bridge may represent a critical juncture in life. You are about to leave one set of conditions and enter a landscape of new possibilities. It could be a new job, a change of home, or a new relationship. It may also represent an inner transformation, such as adopting a new set of values and leaving behind the past.

Mystical Meaning "Life is a bridge across a sea of change. Pass over it but do not build your house on it," says my guru, Sathya Sai Baba. Perhaps the bridge in your dream represents this journey of life.

BROTHER (*SEE ALSO* SHADOW, ANIMA/ANIMUS)

Psychological Meaning Carl Jung claimed that childhood sibling rivalry and jealousy influence the dream symbol of the brother. For a male dreamer, he may represent the shadow side of the personality that is neglected and undeveloped. Sometimes this may include anti-social qualities that are alarming. However, in a woman's dreams a brother may represent the male side of her own personality (animus).

Mystical Meaning A brother may occur as a guide in a woman's dreams and take her into a dark forest, into the depths of the earth, or to the bottom of the sea. This theme, which occurs in many myths and legends, shows that the animus can guide the ego to the cause of a psychological difficulty.

BROWN (*SEE* COLORS)

BRUSH

Psychological Meaning A brush may symbolize your desire to brush away problems. Perhaps you are taking a cavalier attitude to circumstances that need serious consideration? If you dream of sweeping up a mess, you may desire to be pure within or may have a fear of dirty thoughts. (Freud considered brushes to represent pubic hair. Perhaps something in your life needs to be cleaned up?

Mystical Meaning A great deal of superstition is associated with brushes and brooms. It is unlucky to step over them; they can sweep away good luck and are ridden by witches. Generally it is an unlucky symbol, but if you dream of brushing your hair you will soon meet an exciting new partner.

Common Dream

BUILDINGS

My dreams are often set in a small, decaying cellar. I always wake up feeling bad about life when this happens. What does this dream mean? —D.J, Gloucester, England

Psychological Meaning Buildings and houses are symbols of yourself. The upstairs represents your conscious mind and the lower floors and cellar your hidden self.

The cramped feeling of the cellar indicates frustration and a need to expand your activities or thinking. Decayed or crumbling buildings indicate that your self-image has suffered. Treat yourself to a few activities that make you feel good.

Different parts of a house may symbolize different times. For example, modern rooms may represent the conscious mind whereas the oldest areas may represent the ancient mind—the unconscious. The condition of the building may express how you feel about yourself. In addition it can also represent your physical health. Sometimes decayed buildings are the prelude to the onset of an illness.

ASK YOURSELF

1. *What aspect of me does the house represent?* Your mind, body, and spirit? The house may represent how you see yourself. If you recognize the need for a psychological spring cleaning, get to work straightaway.

2. *Is the house symbolic of past circumstances?* For example, your parental home may symbolize your childhood feelings. Ask yourself what personal associations the buildings in your dream have for you.

Mystical Meaning To dream of small buildings spells bad luck, says superstition, but if the building is big you will experience positive changes soon.

BULL

Psychological Meaning The bull is a symbol of male sexuality. For a man, it may represent his own sexuality and virility. For a woman, it may refer to the opposite sex. If the bull in your dreams is wild and untamed, your passions may be out of control. If you dream of bullfighting, it may be symbolic of action to control lust and negative power.

Mystical Meaning In mythology, the bull is an ancient symbol of fertility dating back to earliest times. In the great roar of the storm, man believed he heard the roar of the bull. In the ancient world, the bull was associated with the creative power of spring, as symbolized in the zodiac by Taurus. To dream of a bull has therefore been symbolic of fertility and sexual power since time immemorial.

BURIAL (SEE FUNERAL AND DEATH)

BUSINESS

Psychological Meaning Your dream may be telling you to take a more businesslike attitude to your circumstances. Perhaps you need to sell yourself, or maybe you need to be more cunning, daring, or cautious. Your dream may be showing you ways to profit from your experience. If the business is doing well you may feel pleased with your circumstances at the moment, but business problems may show that you feel insecure at this time.

Mystical Meaning Beware of dishonest people if you dream of a business, say the sages of bygone times.

BUTTERFLY

Psychological Meaning A butterfly may symbolize rebirth, inner beauty, and transformation. It may also represent romance, joy, freedom, and success. It is the essence of your true self.

Mystical Meaning An interesting philosophical question was raised by Chinese philosopher Chuang Chou, who dreamed he was a butterfly. The dream was so vivid, when he awoke he couldn't decide if he was a man dreaming of being a butterfly or a butterfly dreaming of being a man.

BUILDINGS

CACTUS

Psychological Meaning A prickly situation may be symbolized by a cactus. Perhaps you feel needled by someone's remarks or feel you need to defend yourself in some way. Clearly, cacti are also a phallic symbol. Are you afraid of being hurt by a relationship?

Mystical Meaning Mexicans consider cactus an aphrodisiac, so to dream of cactus bodes well for matters of the heart.

CAGE

Psychological Meaning A cage may be an expression of your feelings about being restricted in some way. Perhaps you feel confined by your emotional relationships or you feel that your workplace is like a prison. Part of you desperately wants to escape and feel free again. If you dream of a caged animal, this can show that you hold the instinctive side of yourself in check. You may fear the wild, primitive energies of your nature. Similarly, a caged bird may show your frustrated spiritual ambitions.

Mystical Meaning If you dream of being put into a cage of wild animals, it warns that you are in danger of an accident.

CAKE

Psychological Meaning A cake is usually divided between a number of people and may refer to something that has to be shared. For example, you may feel that you are not getting your fair share of a wage increase at work. Or the cake may refer to your emotional life. A wife, for example may feel that her husband gives too much attention to his work, children, and TV, but that she misses out. Or perhaps you're being selfish. Do you want to eat your cake and have it too?

Mystical Meaning Ancient rites involved making man-shaped cakes, which were eaten to gain the power of the god of the corn. The story of the gingerbread man may have originated from these ancient traditions.

CAMERA

Psychological Meaning This often represents a desire to cling to the past or preserve it forever. However, it may also represent the way you "picture the situation."

Mystical Meaning Undeserved disappointment.

CANDLE

Psychological Meaning A lighted candle may represent the illuminating light of intellect. Similarly, it may symbolize enlightenment or the search for truth via contemplation or meditation. It can also suggest the passage of time and your thoughts about getting older. Freudians consider it to be a phallic symbol, of course.

Mystical Meaning If the flame burns steadily, your friends will support you. If it flickers or goes out, enemies will do you harm. In times past, a whole system of fortune telling was invented based on the flicker of a candle's flame.

CAR

Psychological Meaning Surprisingly, Freud believed that the smooth motion of a car was not a symbol of sexual wish fulfillment. Instead, it represented the progress of psychoanalysis. A car is most likely to represent yourself and your ability to control your life. Are you a good driver in your dream? If so, you may also be steering the right course in life. However, if you drive badly or have an accident, your unconscious may be warning you that you are making mistakes. You may be driving yourself too hard and heading for

---

FAMOUS DREAMER

Francis of Assisi
Saint

Dreams played an important part in the life of St. Francis of Assisi. They gave him the strength to persevere with his life of poverty and establish his order of Franciscan monks. Just before a difficult interview with Pope Innocent III, Francis dreamed he saw a tall tree with wide, thick branches. The nature-loving saint looked upon it with wonder and realized that as he looked he grew in size, until he was the same height as the tree. When he touched its branches, the tree bowed in reverence. Francis took this as a message from God that Pope Innocent III would accept his ideas. He did.

an emotional crash. Maybe someone else is driving the car? You may feel that this person is controlling your life or that the qualities the person represents have unreasonable influence over you. The dream may be expressing your dependence and lack of control.

Mystical Meaning The ancients didn't have cars but they did have carts, and the meaning is much the same. One source claims that to ride a vehicle is a sign that there will be changes at home or in business. If your mode of transport is broken, news from a friend tells of trouble.

CARDS

Psychological Meaning A successful game of cards relies on both luck and skill. Similarly, a successful life depends on these same qualities. Your dream may show that you should use the skills of bluff, strategy, and timing in everyday life. A game such as blackjack may show that it's time to take a chance, whereas a game of patience may show the need for patience in your dealings with others.

Mystical Meaning Diamonds indicate wealth, clubs indicate work, hearts mean you will be happy in love, but spades indicate trouble ahead

CASTLE (*SEE ALSO* BUILDINGS, HOUSE, *AND* MANDALA)

Psychological Meaning A castle represents protection and security. It may also show that your psychological defenses are isolating you from others. It can be a symbol of the self.

Mystical Meaning The castle can represent the mandala, a symmetrical pattern that symbolizes the psyche. For example, in the story of Sleeping Beauty the whole castle sleeps because its masculine and feminine halves cannot relate, resulting in a state of stagnation. The castle is also surrounded by impenetrable thorns, showing that it is as difficult to get to know the inner self as it is to storm a castle.

CASTRATION

Psychological Meaning You may have fears that you have lost your virility or you may feel sexual pressure.

Mystical Meaning The myth of Saturn castrating his father may represent the fear of maturity and the conflicting desire to supplant the father.

CAT

Psychological Meaning Animals represent the instinctive side of your nature. A cat expresses feminine qualities and may represent the positive, creative, and sensuous aspects of femininity. If the cat in your dream is aggressive, it may show that you have problems with the feminine side of yourself. You may be taking a "catty" attitude or may have a negative view of women in general.

Mystical Meaning In mythology, cats were associated with old pagan fertility gods. They were a symbol of the Earth Mother and represented the power and wisdom of nature. Cats were sacred to the Egyptians as custodians of the souls of the dead. Only with the advent of Christianity were they deemed to be the evil familiar of witches. Because of this, most dream books consider it unlucky to dream about cats.

CAVE

Psychological Meaning A cave may represent the womb or female sexuality. What you find within the cave or what comes out of it are the new qualities that the unconscious is giving birth to. The cave may also be the entrance to the ancient mind, where you can discover the wisdom that is latent within you

Mystical Meaning Mythological dragons and monsters often lived in caves and sometimes guarded great treasure in their fiery lair. This is a symbol that shows that first it is necessary to overcome the fear of the unconscious before winning spiritual treasures. In some cases the monster that guards the cave represents a traumatic childhood experience that has been banished from consciousness.

CELLAR

Psychological Meaning Buildings represent the mind, and the cellar represents its deepest levels. It is a dark, damp, and sometimes frightening place where lurk creatures that shun the light of day. A cellar may be the symbolic repository where you discard all the fears and problems you do not want to deal with. In this clandestine world, you will discover your repressed fears, worries, and feelings of guilt and shame. Once you acquaint yourself with these fears and bring them into the light of day, they will no longer have power over you.

Mystical Meaning Superstition says that to dream of a cellar full of wine means you will receive profits from a dubious source.

CEMETERY (SEE DEATH)

CHAINS

Psychological Meaning If you dream of being chained, some part of you is being forcefully held in check. You need to liberate the part of you that wants to express itself. If someone you know is chained, consider what aspect of yourself this person represents. Similarly, if an animal is chained, think about what aspect of your animal nature is being restrained. A bull may represent an aspect of your sexuality, a growling dog may represent your anger, and a chained elephant may show that you are unable to utilize your natural strength and wisdom.

Mystical Meaning Superstition says that to dream of being in chains means that an injustice will be done to you.

CHAMPAGNE

Psychological Meaning A freshly opened bottle of Champagne is often considered to be a symbol of ejaculation and represents the sexual act. Of course it may also symbolize a celebration or a personal achievement that you feel pleased about. The effervescence of Champagne may denote a new burst of creativity or the "bubbly" side of your personality.

Mystical Meaning Dreaming about Champagne forecasts financial difficulties ahead but predicts a happy romance if your dream is set at a wedding reception.

Common Dream

CHASE

My young son has a recurring nightmare of being chased through woods by a shadowy figure. How can I help him overcome his fears?—M.T., Perth, Australia

Psychological Meaning This is a metaphor for insecurity. Circumstances may be closing in on

him, or he may feel at the mercy of feelings that get out of control. He may have feelings of guilt or fear of being caught for something he has done. Ask him if something is upsetting him and reassure him that you will support him whatever it is.

Children who have this dream may be being bullied at school. If the problem persists and you notice unusual or extreme behavior in your child, your child's doctor can put you in touch with someone who can help.

Like dreams of falling, being chased reflects the dreamer's feelings of insecurity. The dreamer is running away from something. According to Freud, men run away from the fear of castration, and women from sexual attackers, which symbolize a woman's secret desire to be wooed.

The figure that pursues the dreamer is most likely to represent an unresolved aspect of the dreamer's circumstances or personality.

ASK YOURSELF

1. *What am I running away from?* You may feel that circumstances are closing in on you and you may feel a need to escape. Perhaps you are being emotionally victimized and you feel vulnerable as you did as a child? Your feelings may be running out of control or there may be something you're avoiding in your external life or inner self. Do you feel guilt?

2. *What am I chasing?* If you are doing the chasing, you are probably trying to banish something from your life. You may be frightened by some aspect of yourself or feel anxiety that you may never reach the goals you have set for yourself.

Mystical Meaning Native Americans believe that if you dream you are being chased, you should face your pursuer, wrestle him to the ground, and then unmask him. Follow this wise counsel and you may discover that your fears are not as terrifying as you thought.

CHEST (SEE ALSO BOX)

Psychological Meaning It is with the chest that you breathe in life-giving air, so the chest may represent the center of your vitality.

Mystical Meaning A large chest warns that you may run into debt, say the auguries of old.

CHASE

CHILD

Psychological Meaning Carl Jung claimed that the dream symbol of a child is a metaphor for the forgotten things in childhood. For example, your dream may be telling you that you've forgotten how to play or should take a more innocent, carefree attitude. The symbol of the child also represents possibilities. It paves the way for future changes in the personality. In addition, the child may represent the part of you that needs reassurance and security.

Mystical Meaning A recurrent theme in mythology is the "divine child." This theme occurs in many mythologies. This mystical figure is often a hero or a savior. For example, the child-hero Hercules strangled two threatening snakes, and the baby Jesus became the Christ who saves humanity from damnation. The divine child is the symbol of the true self, both vulnerable and possessed of great transforming power. In your dream it may represent your divine self growing to its full spiritual potential.

CHRIST

Psychological Meaning The figure of Christ may have many personal associations for you, influenced of course by your attitude to traditional religion. As well as the redeemer, the symbol of Christ can represent perfection of the self, martyrdom, worldly suffering, or resurrection. Perhaps you feel like a martyr or believe you suffer as Christ did on the cross.

Mystical Meaning There are many valid paths to spiritual truth, and the religions of the world express the many ways God is made manifest in people's lives. God is omnipresent and omnipotent and appears in many guises. Perhaps the figure of Christ is using the language of the heart to bring you to God.

CHURCH

Psychological Meaning Churches and other houses of worship stand for the spiritual side of your nature. A building usually represents the dreamer, and a church can therefore symbolize the totally integrated psyche that is centered on what you consider to be supreme truth. It alludes to your core values and the things you deem sacred. Your dream may be making you aware of innate spiritual knowledge and the part of you that is eternal. This dream may be part of a series of dreams in which you explore your inner self and gain insight into divine reality.

Mystical Meaning Holy architecture is usually built according to sacred geometry that symbolizes the unity of the soul with God. In psychological terms, such buildings are mandalas representing the wholeness of the psyche.

CIRCLE (SEE ALSO MANDALA)

Psychological Meaning A circle is the perfect mandala. It represents the perfection of the self and wholeness. You are identifying with the very center of yourself. Hold on to this inner source of strength and well-being.

Mystical Meaning The Chinese consider circles to be good *feng shui*. It is therefore fortunate to dream about them.

CIRCUS (SEE THEATER AND CLOWN)

CITY

Psychological Meaning Cities usually represent community and your social environment, including family and friends. If you dream of visiting a town that feels desolate or you feel isolated from the bustle of activity, it may reflect the way you feel about your role in society. Do you feel rejected by society or by the people around you? Alternatively, if you dream of a walled city it may show that you want to protect yourself from society. You may feel that in your waking life you need to create a little time and space for yourself. A ruined city may show that you are neglecting your social relationships. To dream of being lost shows that you feel you have lost the direction in your own life.

The city may also be a symbol of yourself. Entering the city can symbolize your intention to explore your unconscious. A city on a hill may show your lofty ambition to rise in the world, whereas an underground city or one beneath the sea may symbolize a neglected self.

Mystical Meaning Mythological cities are sometimes pictured having eight gates, with one of them sealed. Each gate represents a turning point in life, and the sealed eighth gate is the final journey of death.

CLIFF (SEE ALSO FALLING)

Psychological Meaning You may be at a critical point in your life and may fear losing control. Emotionally you may feel as if you are teetering on the brink or may feel that your life is like a cliff-hanger movie. If you dream of climbing a cliff, it may show that you are trying to overcome an obstacle. Once you are over this problem, the way ahead should be smooth and even.

Mystical Meaning To dream of climbing a cliff augers well for all projects you undertake.

CLIMBING (SEE ALSO ELEVATOR AND MOUNTAIN)

Psychological Meaning Are you climbing toward a goal or away from something you fear? You may be climbing the ladder of success and feel that something you've wanted for a long time is now nearly within your reach. You have great ambition, but are you confident as you climb or does it fill you with fear? Your unconscious may be reminding you of the adage "Pride goeth before a fall." If you remain sincerely modest despite your success, your friends, family, and colleagues will express pleasure at your success. This will increase the self-confidence you need to reach your goal. However, if you become egotistical and climb too high, eventually someone will knock you down. Most people despise arrogance, but humility wins love.

Walls and mountains to climb symbolize obstacles in life that you need to overcome. An easy climb shows success, but climbing a precarious mountain ledge means that there is an uphill struggle ahead. A meteoric rise to fame is not as easily sustained as a gradual and well-planned rise to prominence. Be cautious and take one step at a time.

Freud considered dreams of climbing to represent a longing for sexual fulfillment.

Mystical Meaning The dream oracles say that to climb a ladder to the last rung means you will succeed in business.

CLOAK

Psychological Meaning To dream of wearing a cloak can represent self-protection or protective warmth and love. Freud considered it a symbol for enveloping female sexuality. A cloak can also designate illicit concealment and secrecy. Are you hiding something from yourself or from the world at large? What is it that you cloak in secrecy?

Mystical Meaning To dream of wearing a cloak forecasts a period of uncertainty ahead. If it has a hood, be warned, for someone you trust is deceiving you.

CLOCK

Psychological Meaning A clock or watch may simply represent the passage of time and indicate whether your dream refers to past, present, or future conditions. It may also show that your life is governed by the artificial routines created by organized society. Perhaps you should live a more carefree lifestyle, less dependent on deadlines or clock watching. A clock can also stand for the human heart and, therefore, the emotional side of your life. A clock showing one minute to midnight may indicate your anxious anticipation about a situation soon to affect you. Similarly, a stopped clock may indicate a stilling of the emotions, while a fast-moving sports watch may show that your emotions are running out of control.

Mystical Meaning To hear a clock chime augers bad news, say the dream oracles.

CLOTHES (SEE ALSO UNDERCLOTHES, NUDITY, THEATER)

Psychological Meaning Clothes can express personality or hide imperfections. The colors of your dream clothes can symbolize your moods. For example, brightly colored clothes may show happiness and optimism, whereas dark clothes may indicate depression and secrets. If the clothes you wear are tattered, then you may need to discard your worn-out attitudes and habits. You may want to redesign yourself and establish a new self-image. You *can* become a new person. To dream of changing your clothes may indicate a change of lifestyle. If your clothes are tight, this can indicate that you feel restricted in some way. You may feel constrained in a relationship, held back at work, or restricted in your professional role.

Mystical Meaning Early dream dictionaries say that to dream of seeing a naked woman is lucky. It foretells that some unexpected honors await you. It was also deemed unlucky to dream of having too many clothes, for this meant you lacked the necessities of life. To dream of new clothes means that you will have a domestic tiff.

CLOUDS

CLOUDS

Psychological Meaning Clouds may represent your moods. White cumulus clouds may represent cheerfulness or spirituality, whereas dark, ominous clouds may represent depression or thunderous anger. Clouds also forecast rain and with it the release of tension.

Mystical Meaning Many mystical traditions advise clearing the "clouds of ignorance" so the light of enlightenment may shine. Similarly, clouds protected the Greek gods who lived on Mount Olympus. Only your intuition can penetrate the highest knowledge.

CLOWN (SEE ALSO HERO/HEROINE)

Psychological Meaning A clown mocks the absurdity of pretentiousness. He is a trickster whom psychologists identify as being a symbol for the first, rudimentary stage in the development of the hero myth—in which the hero is instinctual, uninhibited, and often childish.

Mystical Meaning The Fool in the Tarot cards, who becomes the joker in ordinary playing cards, represents the unconscious side of personality with all its potential for transformation.

COLORS

Psychological Meaning Color can evoke strong emotional responses, and the colors revealed in dreams can tell a great deal about emotional states. Psychologists sometimes use color tests to judge the emotional condition of their patients, and a *feng shui* expert will use color in the home to attract the best energies to bring good fortune. However color meanings can vary from individual to individual, and you may have your own personal associations with a particular color. As with all dream interpretation, trust your own gut feelings.

Red: Red represents passion and sexuality. It can also represent anger or blood—it is the color of the life force.

Orange: Orange is usually associated with balance and healing. It is the passions refined.

Yellow: Often associated with artistic inspiration, yellow is sometimes considered the color of the coward.

Green: The color of nature brings new life and hope. Its negative association is with jealousy.

Blue: Blue is the spiritual color, the color healers have in their auric field. Blue brings harmony and, like the sky, it implies freedom. And, of course, it can sometimes represent depression, as when a person gets the blues.

Purple: This is the color of royalty and profound spiritual knowledge.

Black: Usually a color associated with depression. Time to get rid of those "black" thoughts. It may also indicate unconsciousness.

Brown: The color associated with the earth promises new psychological growth.

White: White is usually a symbol of purity.

Mystical Meaning Psychics see colors in the aura, the energy field that surrounds living things. The dream meaning of colors may relate to the spiritual values traditionally associated with each color. They are: red, sensuality; orange, cleansing; yellow, inspiration; green, recovery; blue, healing; purple, clairvoyance; black, illness; brown, stability; white, spirituality.

COMPASS

Psychological Meaning Your unconscious may be showing you the way. You may need to reconsider the direction your life is going or may need to take time out to get your bearings. This is a hopeful dream that promises to end your feeling of disorientation.

Mystical Meaning In *feng shui*, the eight compass directions symbolize different qualities. South relates to fame, fortune, and recognition or reputation. Southwest relates to marriage, romantic happiness, and partnerships. West relates to children and creativity. Northwest relates to helpful people, mentors, and networking. North relates to career and business success. Northeast relates to knowledge, study, and introspection. East relates to family, elders, authority figures, and health. Southeast relates to wealth and prosperity.

CONFLICT (SEE WAR)

COOKING (SEE ALSO FOOD)

Psychological Meaning If you dream of preparing food for other people, it may indicate that you have a desire to influence others. You may want people to like you or become dependent upon you. Cooking can also symbolize your need to transform a realization of a raw truth or emotion into something more palatable. Finally, the dream may represent your awareness of plans in preparation; i.e., "something's cooking."

Mystical Meaning The dream weavers of old say that to dream of cooking means that many friends will visit you in the future.

CORNER

Psychological Meaning Perhaps you feel frustrated by events that you can do nothing about. You feel trapped. You feel cornered. You are being forced to make a decision and now must take control of the situation. However, to dream of turning a corner suggests that things have taken a turn for the better and you have taken a new, and perhaps better, direction.

Mystical Meaning Corners are usually considered places where negative energy accumulates. You need to be more positive.

CORRIDOR

Psychological Meaning Dreaming of a long corridor that has no end may show that you are desperate to escape a repetitive situation. As well as external troubles, this dream could symbolize repetitive behavior patterns that you need to be free of. In most dreams, corridors represent the passing of one phase of your life to another.

Mystical Meaning In mysticism, corridors and passageways are places where energy moves fast and cannot accumulate. To dream of a corridor may therefore show that you are in danger of losing your energy and vitality.

COUPLE (SEE ALSO ANIMA/ANIMUS)

Psychological Meaning To dream of a couple may symbolize the need to bring together the male and female parts of your psyche.

Mystical Meaning Alchemy was a spiritual tradition that sought spiritual transformation of the psyche. The Royal Couple is one of the main symbols found in *Philosophia Reformata*, written by Mylius in 1622. Their coming together and merging to become one being symbolizes spiritual wholeness.

COW (SEE ALSO MOTHER)

Psychological Meaning Cows nurture, and they are used in dreams to symbolize the mother. Perhaps you are nurturing some new ideas or a part of yourself? For a man, a cow can represent the feminine part of himself. It may also represent an easygoing attitude. Your dream may be telling you to stop rushing around and to start taking your time. Cows also suggest the qualities of dignity, strength, and passive endurance.

Mystical Meaning Cows are sacred to the Hindus because they symbolize the protective, nurturing aspect of the godhead. Krishna taught the cow herders not to worship an unseen god, but their own cows. "There is where your devotion is, and where God's blessing to you resides. Worship your cows!" The lesson is clear that "God is your highest concern."

CROCODILE

Psychological Meaning Perhaps the crocodile is you? Are you being snappy all the time? The crocodile can be a symbol of aggressiveness and the shadowy realm of the instincts. Alternatively, the dream may reveal that you have been displaying false emotions and shedding "crocodile tears" or that someone close to you has.

Mystical Meaning To dream of a crocodile was believed to mean that your best friends would deceive you.

CROSS (SEE ALSO MANDALA)

Psychological Meaning The cross was used as a symbol even before the Christian era. The Greek cross, with its four arms of equal length, is a mandala of wholeness. Similarly, Native Americans drew crosses to symbolize the quartering of the universe into active and passive units. As a Christian symbol, it can represent suffering, martyrdom, death, and sacrifice. Perhaps your dream is telling you that you have a cross to bear. Find out what it is that makes you suffer, and begin healing this condition that brings you so much pain. Similarly, the cross also indicates resurrection. The ego must be sacrificed on the cross so that you can rise to God-consciousness.

Mystical Meaning In mysticism, the cross symbolizes the fourfold divisions of nature, such as seasons, the four compass directions, and elements. In the ancient world, it was considered the ideal shape of man, the blueprint of his nature. It is also closely associated with the life-giving power of the tree.

CROSSROADS

Psychological Meaning Your life has come to a crisis point and you must now choose between a number of options. Each road represents a direction you can travel in your life at this time. The choice may be difficult and painful, but you must make your decision.

Mystical Meaning Criminals were hanged at crossroads so that the maximum number of travelers would witness the consequences of crime. As a dream symbol the crossroads can therefore represent crime, punishment, and death. However, most old dream books say that dreaming of a crossroads means an important decision ahead.

CROW

Psychological Meaning The crow may represent the dark part of your psyche that appears at first to be frightening but contains what you need for spiritual enrichment. Crows, like angels, were once believed to be the messengers of the gods. In your dream, they are messengers from your unconscious.

Mystical Meaning Associated with witchcraft, the crow is said to have the gift of prophecy. Some people believe that dreams that include crows foretell future events.

CROWD

Psychological Meaning Your dream may be telling you that you need to make some space for yourself. You need solitude occasionally to reflect on events. In these moments of quiet meditation you can recharge your energy and gain a clearer insight into what it is you truly want from life. Dreaming about a crowd may show that the worries and the problems of the world are pressing in on you.

Mystical Meaning Old dream books say it is fortunate to dream of a crowd as long as they are well dressed or wearing brightly colored clothes. It means many friends will come your way.

CRYSTAL

Psychological Meaning The mathematical symmetry of a crystal can represent unity and wholeness. The crystal may represent the quintessence of your self. It is the pure spirit, the divine cosmic plan unfolding in human form. It is the eternal part of you, unsullied by the world. If you dream of gazing into a crystal, this can show that you are looking within yourself to find your true destiny.

Mystical Meaning Crystals are associated with the healing powers of the spirit. Their vibrations resonate with the life force within the aura and bring peace, harmony, and health. To dream of a crystal reveals that these hidden potentials are also within you.

CUP

Psychological Meaning The cup is considered to be a classic female sexual symbol. It may also represent something passive from which you can draw sustenance. If the cup contains wine, your dream may have a spiritual message.

Mystical Meaning The dream may be referring to the Holy Grail and the search for spiritual sustenance. A cup can also stand for love and truth. For example, the Tarot card suit of cups symbolizes the inquirer's emotional life and is generally a fortunate augury.

CUPBOARD (SEE ALSO CLOTHES, MOTHER, MASK)

Psychological Meaning A Freudian psychologist will tell you that cupboards represent the mother and show your desire to return to the secure waters of your mother's womb. However, it may simply represent something you open in order to reveal a truth. Perhaps a skeleton is hidden in the cupboard—something about yourself you do not want to accept or reveal. As a cupboard may contain clothes, the dream may be telling you about the side of yourself you present to the world (your persona).

Mystical Meaning Dream superstition tells that if you dream of an empty cupboard you will be poor, but if it is full, good fortune will not desert you.

CURTAIN

Psychological Meaning To dream of opening curtains can show your readiness to look at what has been hidden, whereas closing curtains may show a desire to hide or repress your feelings. Theater curtains can represent the beginning or ending of something. Death has sometimes been called "the final curtain." Perhaps your behavior has been a bit of a performance, but now you've changed your ways?

Mystical Meaning Tradition has it that to dream of curtains means that an unwelcome visitor will arrive. There may be quarrels.

CUTTING

Psychological Meaning To cut is to sever and separate. Your dream may be an allegory for a broken relationship, a major change in your circumstances, or the end of an outmoded pattern of behavior.

Mystical Meaning Dream oracles tell that to dream of being cut means that a friend will betray you.

DAFFODIL (SEE ALSO MANDALA AND COLORS)

Psychological Meaning Associated with the springtime, daffodils are a symbol of renewal. This is a time of inner growth, optimism, and hope. The beautiful symmetry of flowers is reminiscent of mandalas, which can symbolize psychological wholeness. The color yellow is sometimes associated with the sun and the light of inspiration.

Mystical Meaning According to a Celtic tradition from the country of Wales, a bunch or field of daffodils means more gold than silver will come your way, but a single bloom brings misfortune.

DAGGER (SEE KNIFE)

DAM

Psychological Meaning To dream of a dam may mean that you have some pent-up emotions that need to be released. If you dream of a dam bursting, it shows that you have lost control. Your anger may have gone beyond the point of self-control. You may feel overwhelmed with emotion. There is more than one way to deal with frustrations. Be kinder to yourself and others and honestly express your feelings in a controlled and gentle way.

Mystical Meaning Victorian dream books interpret blockages, impediments, and obstacles as prophecies forecasting problems ahead that must be overcome. Dams fall into this category.

DANCE

Psychological Meaning Dance is usually a celebratory activity, something you do when you feel happy. This dream may therefore indicate that you feel pleased about the way a situation is progressing at the moment. You may feel a sense of freedom from constraining influences. Other things may also be expressed by dance. For example, if you dance with another person, this intimacy can represent sexual intercourse. A man and woman dancing together may show the union of the masculine and feminine aspects of your personality (see Anima/Animus).

Mystical Meaning To dream of dancing can be a mystical symbol. It can, for example, represent the eternal dance of the Hindu god Shiva, who symbolizes the eternal movement of time and the powers of creation and destruction.

DARKNESS

Psychological Meaning Light is a symbol of awareness. Darkness is the absence of light and therefore is a symbol of the unconscious. If you react with fear, you may fear the unconscious, but if the darkness is comforting, you accept this unknown part of yourself. If you dream of being lost in darkness it may represent your feelings of desperation, depression, or insecurity. If you see light, it may show that you are being guided toward wholeness and understanding.

Mystical Meaning The Chinese oracle of the *I Ching* used by Carl Jung as an aid to interpreting dreams says of darkness: "In the end it perishes of its own darkness, for evil must itself fall at the very moment when it has wholly overcome the good, and thus consumed the energy to which it owed its duration." In other words, things can only get better.

DAWN

Psychological Meaning The dawn brings with it a new beginning. A period of inner darkness is replaced by the light of realization and consciousness. At last you have hope and optimism in your heart.

Mystical Meaning The ancient Egyptians identified dawn with New Year's Day and the beginning of the world, when the eye of Atum searched the great primeval ocean. Since the earliest times humanity has worshiped the rising sun as a symbol of God, hope, and rebirth.

Common Dream

DEATH (SEE ALSO FUNERAL)

I dreamed that I was dead and everyone stood around me crying. I awoke with a feeling of abject horror. Is this dream a prediction of my death?—Jose T., Quebec, Canada

Psychological Meaning Dreams of death represent the ending of one phase so a new one can begin. They can show forthcoming finalities, such as the end of a marriage or career. These are symbolic dreams and are unlikely to forecast an actual event. If the dead person is someone you know, consider what aspect of yourself that person represents. For example, to dream of your mother dying could represent the death of the motherly side of your own nature. Perhaps you should try to be more caring and maternal, or perhaps plans you have should be nurtured rather than killed off. Alternatively, you may also be expressing your hidden feelings about the person. Do you secretly resent the person or have a desire to be independent of him or her? Dead animals may also represent aspects of yourself. They indicate that you may be rejecting or repressing your instinctive side.

Freud believed that everyone has two contending basic drives: *eros*, which is the drive toward pleasure and life, and *thanatos*, the drive toward death. If the dead person in your dream was yourself, you may want to consider the following:

ASK YOURSELF

1. *What is being expressed in the dream?* Perhaps you fear dying, and the dream is reminding you of your own mortality? It is healthy to accept that death comes to everyone; this realization broadens your spiritual perspective and loosens the grip of material craving. Everything in the world is the dust of stars, but look deep within yourself and you may find the part of yourself that is eternal.

2. *Am I trying to free myself from something?* You may want to leave your old self behind so a new you can be reborn. Free yourself of emotional burdens and open yourself to new potentials. There is no need to be a martyr. The way forward is to establish a new set of values that are beneficial to you and others.

3. *Do I feel suicidal?* There's no need to punish yourself or others because of how you feel. Everyone occasionally feels a desire to retreat from life's problems or from feelings of failure. But suffering is a blessing as well as a curse. It is through adversity that you grow and become a better person. Be like a strong tree that bends with the wind but never breaks. Better times will inevitably come again.

Mystical Meaning To dream of meeting dead people you once knew is part of the grieving process. Sometimes the feeling of loss is symbolized by being rejected, divorced, or attacked by the person you loved. You may dream that they ignore you or have traveled far away. This is all part of the process of coming to terms with the death of a loved one. However, there are some dreams that cannot be explained as symbolism, allegory, or metaphor. From the many casebooks I have collected, it appears that occasionally the dead can communicate with the living through dreams. I have cases on file where information has been given to the dreamer that could not have been known other than by paranormal means. For example, one woman wrote to say that her dead husband told her exactly where to find the missing will, and I have many instances recorded where the dead person has announced his passing via a dream.

DESCENT

Psychological Meaning In many dreams this may represent descending into the unconscious. In particular, cave entrances, wells, tombs, and cellars can represent entrances to the netherworld of the unconscious. Alternatively, you may interpret this as a downward phase in your life; you may feel "down." On the other hand, perhaps you are over the worst and everything is downhill from now on.

Mystical Meaning Legend has it that the people of ancient Crete built temples in underground caves. Here they held their strange rituals and bull-dancing ceremonies. Since the earliest times, the descent into the underground world has been a symbol of man's search for divinity and spiritual empowerment.

DETECTIVE

Psychological Meaning In real life, detectives seek out hidden truths. During sleep, you may be trying to resolve a problem and may want to know the truth about an issue that worries you. Perhaps you detect that something is wrong or that someone has been less than honest with you.

Mystical Meaning To dream of being falsely accused of a crime by a detective is a dream prophecy that fortune and honor are coming your way.

DEVIL

Psychological Meaning The devil in your dream may personify your fear or repressed desires that have been buried in the underworld of the unconscious. In reality, the unconscious mind is not full of evil demons and satanic forces; it is your inner resource that gives energy and wisdom. Your own fear of the unknown prevents you from finding the wholeness and healing that the unconscious offers. Alternatively, the Devil may symbolize evil words and deeds that you or others have been displaying in waking life. What the devil fears most is light and love. Honesty and kindness may be the right form of conduct to overcome the perceived evils that trouble you.

Mystical Meaning The figure of Satan occurs in the Jewish, Christian, and Islamic traditions. Originally Satan represented fertility and the powers of Nature. Similarly, the cloven-footed god Pan of the ancient Greeks was a god of the abundance of nature. These ancient symbols of fertility are sometimes used by the unconscious to show the inauguration of a new phase of psychological growth.

DIRT

Psychological Meaning Do you have a feeling of disgust? Dreaming of dirt could represent your emotional reaction to your instincts or self-disgust about sexuality. You may have guilt feelings that could originate from childhood. Society places too great an emphasis on sex. Accept it as a natural. It's not dirty, but also is not necessarily the all-important issue of life.

Mystical Meaning Earth and soil can represent the alchemists' *prima materia*, the unconscious content worked with in order to become enlightened.

DISEASE

Psychological Meaning Sometimes dreams spot an illness before you are aware of any symptoms. If your dream persists, get your health checked by your doctor. Alternatively, the dream may be highlighting anxieties and inner conflicts. You need to heal these inner troubles and find psychological harmony. If someone else in your dream has a disease, you may either harbor hostile feelings or fear for the person's mental equilibrium.

Mystical Meaning African superstition has simple interpretation to this one: see your witch doctor for a cure.

DISGUISE (SEE ALSO MASK)

Psychological Meaning It is likely that you're hiding from something in your waking life. You want to "dress up" an issue and turn it into something it's not. It's time to face reality and stop hiding behind that mask. Be yourself.

Mystical Meaning Many myths and children's stories tell of people who wear masks but then to their horror realize that they can't remove them.

This is a symbol that shows that you can sometimes become the person you pretend to be but forget who you really are.

DIVING

Psychological Meaning Water and the sea often represent the unconscious. Diving into water symbolizes your descent into the unconscious. You are getting in touch with the deepest strata of your being. Alternatively, the dream may be telling you to take a chance concerning an issue from waking life. It's time to take the plunge.

Mystical Meaning There are many myths that tell of heroes who dive to the bottom of the sea and bring up great treasure. In dreams, this represents the ego descending into the unconscious and finding the self.

DIVORCE

Psychological Meaning The dream may represent a hidden desire on your part to end a relationship. You may feel unhappy about your marriage or partner. Perhaps you should express your concerns and make your unhappiness known. A good relationship is both giving and taking, so don't just make demands. Look for solutions that bring happiness to both of you.

Mystical Meaning The old dream oracles wisely advised that this dream was a warning and that you should cultivate a more congenial domestic atmosphere.

DOG

Psychological Meaning Dogs helped man hunt and herd his flock. They are therefore a symbol of the right inner relationship between you and your animal nature. They may also symbolize loyalty and guidance. Alternatively, if the dog is ferocious, you have an inner conflict with the animal side of your nature. A dog straining on its leash may indicate that your emotions are at the end of their tether. Perhaps you need to express your anger about an issue that upsets you.

Mystical Meaning One dream oracle warns that to dream of a bloodhound is an omen for your imminent downfall. You'd be barking mad to believe that.

DOLL

Psychological Meaning To dream of playing with dolls may symbolize that you are trying to come to terms with an infantile aspect of yourself. This can sometimes indicate a lack of communication between the conscious and unconscious levels of the mind. It can symbolize that you have an immature attitude toward the opposite sex. Are you behaving like an adult, or do you sometimes resort to childish behavior? Alternatively, Jung believed that dolls represented the Anima or Animus, the qualities of the opposite sex within yourself.

Mystical Meaning Tribal magicians use mannequins to inaugurate their sympathetic magic. Sticking pins into a voodoo doll of your enemy, telling your troubles to a worry doll, and worshiping the corn doll are rituals that express a multitude of needs, desires, fears, and hopes. Children will confess to a doll things they would never tell an adult. Similarly, you may tell the doll of your dream your most secret fears and wishes.

DOLPHIN

Psychological Meaning Dolphins that leap in and out of the sea may represent communication between the unconscious and the conscious mind.

Mystical Meaning There will be a change of government!

DOOR

Psychological Meaning If a door opens outward, it may show that you have a need to be more accessible to others. However, an inward-opening door may represent your desire for inner exploration and self-discovery. A door may also represent a new opening in your waking life or a desire to open up your feelings. If the door is locked, you may feel that opportunities are being denied you, or alternatively it can represent closing the door to the past.

Mystical Meaning There are lots of dream oracles for this one: a doorknob means unexpected good luck; hinges bring family problems; locked doors show missed opportunities; an open door predicts good fortune; a revolving door means a monotonous period ahead; and a trapdoor predicts shocking news.

DRAGON

Psychological Meaning The dragon sometimes guards the entrance to a cave full of treasure. It symbolizes the fears you must overcome before realizing the true self. Sometimes the dragon can represent a guardian of the spirit. A Freudian psychologist interprets the dragon symbol to represent the devouring aspect of the mother. It is the resistance that prevents a man from realizing the feminine aspect of his nature. Your dream could also be saying something about your sex drive. Dragons have a strong association with fire and, therefore, passion.

Mystical Meaning In China, the symbol of the dragon is quite different from its Western counterpart. It has amazing power, is highly spiritual, and symbolizes the wisdom of the mind. To dream about dragons is very auspicious.

DRAWING

Psychological Meaning The dream may simply mean that you may have latent artistic abilities that should be given expression. Are you drawing on inner resources, or is your bank account overdrawn? What you draw is also important, as it can show the plans, problems, and worries that you are trying to resolve.

Mystical Meaning A strange superstition says that if a woman dreams of drawing with a pencil and then rubs out what she drew, her lover will be unfaithful.

DROWNING

DROWNING

Psychological Meaning Dreams of drowning or struggling in treacherous waters may represent your fear of being swallowed by forces hidden in the depths of your unconscious. You may be proceeding too quickly in opening your unconscious. It may be helpful to talk your problems and fears through with a friend who can throw you a lifeline and help you keep your head above water. The dream also shows that you are overwhelmed by your emotions. You may fear sinking financially, or you may be drowning in your difficulties. Do you feel that in your waking life you are being sucked into something you would rather not be a part of? Pause for a while and make sure you have your feet firmly on solid ground before you make any major decision.

Mystical Meaning A business will founder if you dream of drowning but will succeed if you are rescued.

DRUNK

Psychological Meaning Are you intoxicated by your own success or do you want to escape from reality? The dream suggests that you are not seeing your circumstances clearly and need to take a more sober view of things.

Mystical Meaning The Gypsies believe that if you dream you see a drunk you will be given a small but pleasant surprise.

DUEL

Psychological Meaning It is likely you are experiencing an inner conflict. You need to find a middle way between the extreme views and the solutions you are considering. Similarly, the conflict could be between your conscious thoughts and your instinctive feelings. You will not know peace until you stop this inner conflict. Stop seeing things only in black and white. A compromise is necessary.

Mystical Meaning Children's stories and fairy tales often illustrate psychological processes and are rich in dream symbols. In Lewis Carroll's *Through the Looking Glass*, Tweedledum and Tweedledee typify the childlike inner conflicts that can occur within the psyche.

DUMB

Psychological Meaning To dream of a person who is unable to speak or who refuses to speak represents an undeveloped function within the self. Psychologist Carl Jung said that these silent figures represent an imbalance between emotion and intellect. One side of the personality overpowers the other, rendering it speechless or impotent. Some people suffer from sleep paralysis. They wake up before the back part of the brain has started to function. This area stops the body from acting out dreams and prevents the dreamer from thrashing around while sleeping. The dreamer may "wake up" but be completely paralyzed. If this happens to you, you may want to speak, cry out, or scream but find that you can't. Don't panic. Relax until your whole brain starts working.

Mystical Meaning To dream of being dumb means that you are unable to convince people of the worth of your plans. However, a dumb person who dreams of being dumb must beware of false friends!

DUST

Psychological Meaning Dust implies neglect and something that has not been touched for a long time. Your dream therefore represents aspects of yourself that have been ignored or forgotten. It could be an ambition from the past or something you once treasured but have until now overlooked. Is the whole of your personality being expressed in your waking life? Similarly, it may be a neglected talent, such as an artistic, musical, or creative ability, that the dream draws your attention to. The objects covered in dust will give you a clue to the dream's meaning.

Mystical Meaning The Gypsies say that the more dust you see in a dream, the more minor irritations you will need to deal with.

DWARF

Psychological Meaning A dwarf can represent some quality that you have not fully developed or expressed. It may also represent the neglected or repressed parts of yourself—aspects of your personality that were unable to grow to their full potential.

Mystical Meaning Gold is a symbol of the true self and, as in the story of Snow White, is often mined by dwarfs. Dwarfs can therefore symbolize your quest for self-knowledge.

EAGLE

Psychological Meaning The eagle is a powerful bird that may represent powerful intellectual or spiritual abilities. For a Christian it may represent John the Evangelist, and for an American it may be the symbol of your country.

Mystical Meaning Early man considered eagles messengers from the sun god. In a dream, an eagle may be a messenger from your unconscious. Mythology often has stories of the eagle and the lion or the eagle and the snake. These stories are dream symbols that represent psychological opposites such as spiritual/animal, male/female, conscious/unconscious, and thought/instinct. Superstition says that to dream of an eagle is an omen for fame and fortune.

EAR

Psychological Meaning An ear may be telling you to listen to what you are being told. The advice may be coming from people you know in waking life or from your own inner self. Perhaps you should listen to the voice of your conscience?
Mystical Meaning You will hear news soon, but if your ears ache, do not trust the person who tells you.

EARTH

Psychological Meaning Dreams associated with the earth, such as lying on the ground, may show that you need to be realistic. The dream may be telling you to keep your feet on the ground. You may need to concentrate on earthly matters rather than becoming overly involved in otherworldly concerns or flights of fancy. To dream of the planet Earth may be a symbol of your true self that is yet unrealized. Sometimes, dreams are not symbolic, but can be real experiences of paranormal travel. Psychologist Carl Jung in his autobiography, *Memories Dreams Reflections,* confesses that in 1944 he had an out-of-body experience and saw the Earth from a vantage point in space. "It seemed to me that I was high up in space. Far below I saw the globe of the earth, bathed in gloriously blue light."

Mystical Meaning Mother Earth represents the unconscious mind. She is the womb that contains potential for further development. Myths about descending into the earth are allegories to describe the descent into the dark realms of the unconscious. If Mother Earth comes in a fearful guise, this may show that you fear being overwhelmed by chaotic unconscious forces that threaten the order in your life. Mother Earth was of course a fertility symbol. To dream of a barren earth means that you need to sow new seeds of life for the future.

EARTHQUAKE

Psychological Meaning Something is upsetting you that has destroyed your feeling of security. You may feel that your whole world is falling apart. You may "quake" with fear. Similarly, something may be threatening you from below the surface of your awareness. It may be repressed fear or anxiety that you have pushed underground into the depths of your unconscious.
Mystical Meaning Dream superstition interprets earthquakes as a symbol of a change of circumstance.

EAST

Psychological Meaning The sun rises in the East. This direction may therefore represent a new dawn and rebirth. You may also be interested in the philosophy and spiritual wisdom that comes from the great cultures of the East.
Mystical Meaning Your plans will be canceled, say the old dream superstitions.

EATING (SEE ALSO FOOD)

Psychological Meaning Freud considered the mouth to be the primary erogenous zone. Dreams of eating are therefore closely associated with sexuality. If you dream of gorging yourself, it can indicate that you have an indulgent sexuality, whereas dreaming of fasting or starvation may indicate that you deny your sexual needs. Eating out at restaurants is often part of couples' courting rituals. In dreams, meals that have an enjoyable atmosphere reflect a confirmation of intimacy with others and good social relationships. Dreaming of eating in uncomfortable or threatening surroundings may represent frigidity and unhappiness with your relationships. An alternative explanation is that eating symbolizes qualities that you are making part of yourself. For example, you may be digesting some new ideas or perhaps a problem is "eating at you."

Mystical Meaning To dream of eating generally warns of a quarrel or business loss. Seers claim that it is particularly bad to dream of eating salt or lard, as these signify a serious argument.

ECLIPSE (*SEE* MOON)

EGG (*SEE ALSO* SHELLS)

Psychological Meaning To dream of an egg promises that something new is about to happen in your life. You may be "hatching" a new idea or plan. After a period of waiting, wonderful new possibilities will open to you. At this stage you will need to carefully nurture your plans, as eggs are delicate things and can be easily broken. The egg could also symbolize inner potential that is developing within you. You may be learning new skills or feel that you are developing into a new and better person. You need time to incubate this new side of yourself. Soon you will be able to break out of your shell.

Mystical Meaning According to the *Oneirocriticon*, by Astrampsychus (c. 350 A.D.), "to hold an egg symbolizes vexation."

ELEMENTS (*SEE ALSO* AIR, EARTH, FIRE, WATER)

Psychological Meaning The elements are symbols for the sum total of the universe, including man. These are divided into solid (Earth), liquid (Water), and vapor (Air) and these three are transformed into one another through the agency of energy (Fire). Psychological qualities can be represented by each of the elements. If these are in balance, then it represents psychological wholeness and well-being.

Mystical Meaning In astrology the elements symbolize the four essential qualities of mankind: Earth, for fertility and steadfastness; Water, for imagination; Air, for intelligence; and Fire, for ambition and will. In addition, the mystics believed in a fifth element called Ether, an intangible fluid state of existence that alchemists claimed permeated everything. Today, many psychics believe that ether is the medium by which the spirit travels out of the body during sleep.

ELEPHANT

Psychological Meaning Elephants can symbolize inner strength and wisdom. They may also represent memory. Jung believed they represented the self. The defensive nature of an elephant may represent an introverted nature.

Mystical Meaning To a Hindu the elephant-headed god Ganesha represents God's power to remove obstacles. Similarly, Western dream interpretation has always considered dreams of elephants to bring great good luck.

ELEVATOR (*SEE ALSO* LIFT)

Psychological Meaning You may feel that you are going up in the world. As no effort is required to make your ascent, you may feel that someone is helping you or that destiny is working in your favor. You may also have raised your consciousness and may see the world from an elevated standpoint. As you transcend the lower planes and perhaps become more cerebral in your thinking, remember not to lose touch with your instinctive and intuitive nature. If the elevator is descending, it can indicate the descent of the conscious ego into the unconscious in order to explore this hidden world. Alternatively, it may represent the decline of your personal power and status. In both instances, remember it's who you are, not what you are, that counts.

Mystical Meaning They didn't have elevators in the good old days. However, it was always considered a good omen to dream to make an ascent without any obstacles and without stumbling.

EMBARRASSMENT

Psychological Meaning Dreams often expose your hidden weaknesses and fears. You may feel that your self-confidence has been undermined, or you may feel insecure about your sexuality.

Mystical Meaning Some old dream superstitions say that dreams represent the opposite of what they appear to mean. In this case, the greater the embarrassment you feel, the greater your success will be!

EMOTIONS (*SEE ALSO* SHADOW)

Psychological Meaning Some psychologists believe that people dream in order to allow the emotions to settle down. Without dreams, you would simply overheat. Dreams can sometimes express very powerful emotions, ones that most people wouldn't dare express in waking life. Dreams can act as an emotional safety valve to help release tension. Jung pointed out that emotions come from the "Shadow," the undeveloped, inferior functions of the psyche. Many people refuse to recognize these emotions as their own and project them onto someone else.

Mystical Meaning Some superstitions say to reverse the emotional meaning of the dream. For example, to dream of being angry or crying means that you will soon hear some good news.

EMPTY

Psychological Meaning You feel that something is missing in your life. To dream of an empty room, box, house, or vessel may be to express feelings of emotional emptiness. Freud believed that these feelings were the result of repression.

Mystical Meaning Ventures undertaken at this time will be futile, say the dream oracles.

ENEMY

Psychological Meaning The enemy may be the enemy within. Do you have inner conflicts that need resolving? You may have rejected parts of yourself that are struggling with you to find expression. The shadow side of yourself may contain the qualities you need for personal wholeness. Alternatively the enemy may represent problems with a real-life enemy and your dream may give you clues to reconciliation.

Mystical Meaning They say that if you dream of enemies, it means you will have helpful friends.

ESCAPE (SEE ALSO CHASE)

Psychological Meaning You may want to escape from a restrictive attitude or situation that is preventing your psychological growth. Alternatively, you may be taking an escapist attitude and refusing to face up to problems that continue to pursue you.

Mystical Meaning The oracles say: A man who dreams of trying to escape from danger will soon face serious trouble.

ETHER (SEE ELEMENTS)

EVIL

Psychological Meaning Everyone has a dark side. The evil that occurs in dreams usually represents something about yourself. It may represent destructive psychological forces such as anger, jealousy, revenge, or hatred. If you recognize these tendencies within yourself, first accept them, then practice the opposite in waking life. For example, if you dream of hatred, practice love; if you dream of revenge, practice forgiveness; and if you dream of jealousy, practice giving.

Mystical Meaning The ancient Chinese oracle the *I Ching*, often used for dream interpretation, says: "The best way to overcome evil is by energetic perseverance in the good"

EXAMINATION

Psychological Meaning Dreaming of sitting for an examination may express a fear of failure. Examinations are very stressful experiences in which you are made to face up to your shortcomings. To dream of failing an exam, being late for one, or being unprepared shows that you feel unprepared for the challenges of waking life. Do not fear failure. Always do your very best and you will never have regrets.

Mystical Meaning Ancient dream guides tell that to dream of passing an examination forecasts success in life, but that failing an exam means failing in life. However, other sources say that to dream of failure augers success. So who knows what the correct answer to this dream interpretation is?

EXCREMENT

Psychological Meaning Excrement represents something you need to be rid of. This may be a negative attitude, an outdated mode of behavior, or destructive influence from the past. Rid yourself of these negative emotions. Alternatively, practical worries in waking life may make you feel like you've put your foot in it.

Mystical Meaning If you dream of treading in dog's mess while walking down the street, it means you'll have unexpected good luck financially. (You'll be stinking rich!)

EXPLOSION (SEE BOMB)

EYES

Psychological Meaning These "windows to the soul" give clues to the state of your spiritual health and well-being. Bright eyes suggest a healthy inner life. They may also represent insight or psychic awareness. The eye can be a symbol of wisdom and clear perception of your circumstances. It can show your way of looking at things. Are the eyes happy, sad, kind, judgmental, or enlightened? The nature of the eye may say a great deal about the way you perceive your circumstances. For example, a green eye may symbolize that you have feelings of jealousy. If you dream of the evil eye, this can represent your super-ego, the internal censor that passes judgment on your thoughts and desires. In extreme cases, to dream of a sinister eye may indicate that you harbor feelings of paranoia.

Mystical Meaning Within mystical traditions, eyes are considered to be a symbol of higher consciousness. It is believed that people have a third eye just above the eyebrows, in the center of the forehead. This spiritual center can perceive other dimensions and spiritual realities. Directly in line with this center, in the middle of the brain, lies the pineal gland, which releases chemicals that may control higher consciousness. It is believed that this was once an eye, and that over the centuries it became buried in the center of the brain. The Tuatara lizard of New Zealand still has a vestigial eye at to the top of the head that is sensitive to light.

FACE (SEE ALSO MASK)

Psychological Meaning If you dream of your own face it may represent the face you show to the world as opposed to the real you. This is particularly the case if you dream of putting on makeup. The dream may also contain puns. For example, are you "facing up" to your problems, or should you address an enemy "face-to-face"?

Mystical Meaning The dream oracles say that to dream of seeing your face in a mirror means that a secret will be discovered. If your face is swollen, you will receive money but if it is pale, disappointment will follow.

FAILURE

Psychological Meaning Fear of failure may originate in childhood and stem from fears of punishment or withdrawal of love. Failure themes can occur in dreams about missing trains, muddled words, or failing an examination. Too many people program themselves with failure habits. Instead of focusing on where you go wrong, emphasize the things you get right. Give yourself permission to succeed.

Mystical Meaning If you dream of failing in business or love, you will succeed in both, say the dream books of bygone days.

FAIRY

Psychological Meaning Fairy tales are full of rich psychological symbolism, and telling them can help children and adults express their innermost fears and hopes. For a man a fairy may symbolize the female aspect of his personality that can be integrated for better psychic balance. Similarly, for a woman a fairy may represent either her femininity or her motherly side.

Mystical Meaning Some cultures believe that fairies are real beings that tend and direct the powers of nature. The Findhorn organization calls them Devas and may have proved their existence by demonstrating that barren land can be made to bloom by calling for faireis' help. In dreams, it may actually be possible to communicate with these elemental powers.

FALLING

Common Dream

Many times as I'm going to sleep, I dream that I am walking along the road and suddenly trip up and fall toward the pavement. I always wake up before I hit the ground. Why do I dream this?—J.H., London, England

Psychological Meaning Dreams about falling usually occur as you are "falling off" to sleep. They may be triggered by a drop in blood pressure, a movement of the fluid in the middle ear, or a limb dangling off the side of the bed.

Some psychologists believe that these are archaic memories from the time when the ancestors of humans were tree-dwelling primates. The ape-men that survived their fall passed on their genes with the memory of the event. The dead ones did not. And that's why so often you dream of falling but of never hitting the ground.

As a symbol, falling highlights a loss of emotional equilibrium or self-control. You may fear "letting go" in real life. Anxiety usually accompanies this dream. It may represent your insecurity, a lack of self-confidence, a fear of failure, or an inability to cope with a situation. There could also be a literal interpretation. You may have noticed something unsafe—a loose stair rail, a wobbly ladder, or an insecure window. Check it out. The dream may be a warning.

ASK YOURSELF

1. *Am I over-ambitious?* Perhaps you have climbed above your station and are experiencing the pride before a fall? You may have to lower your sights somewhat and set yourself goals that are more realistic.

2. *Do I fear letting go?* The dream may be urging you to stop resisting an impulse from the unconscious. Psychologist Strephon Kaplan-Williams suggests that you relive the dream in your imagination and let the fall complete itself. In this way, you will find out what is frightening you and get to the bottom of the problem.

Mystical Meaning Some sources claim that if you dream of falling into mud, someone has told lies about you. Other dreams about falling forecast monetary loss.

FAMOUS

Psychological Meaning People who appear in your dreams represent aspects of your own self that you may be unaware of. Famous people usually represent the person you would like to be. Ask yourself what psychological characteristics and traits this person symbolizes for you. These may be the qualities that you need to integrate into your own personality. If you dream of being famous yourself, it may show your need to be admired by the people around you.

Mystical Meaning It is said that to dream of being famous means that you are trying to grasp something beyond your reach.

FATHER (*SEE ALSO* MOTHER)

Psychological Meaning As an archetype, the father represents the protector, lawgiver, or ruler. He may appear in dreams as a king, emperor, wise old man, or as the sun, a weapon, or a phallus. Jung considered this important symbol to play a crucial psychological role in the destiny of the individual. Sometimes this figure may represent the conscience and show your conventional moral opinions. If the father plays the role of protector, it may symbolize the need to become more self-reliant and depend on your own resources. Many people dream of hostility toward their father. This shows that the unconscious is dethroning the father in order to enable you to achieve a proper sense of yourself and be a person in your own right.

Mystical Meaning Freud considered the ancient Greek myth of Oedipus to symbolize the psychological development of an individual. He claimed that failure to achieve freedom from parental influence resulted in an Oedipus complex. Children (usually between four and seven years old) go through a phase where they develop an incestuous desire for the parent of the opposite sex. The complex occurs when the young boy has feelings of resentment toward his father, whom he sees as his rival. Perhaps the father may punish him by castration? Normally the Oedipus complex resolves itself before puberty.

FEAR

Psychological Meaning Bad memories, feelings of guilt, self-doubt, worries, anger, desires, insecurities, and anxieties are often pushed out of your waking thoughts and repressed. Nightmares occur when these hidden fears force you to pay attention to them. This is an opportunity to discover what part of you is threatening to destroy your inner peace. What is it that you fear so much that you have to push it away into the darkness of the unconscious?

Mystical Meaning The superstitions come close to modern psychology with this one: If you overcome whatever frightens you in your dreams, you will also overcome the things that frighten you in waking life.

FEAST

Psychological Meaning You have the emotional need to gorge yourself. This may not necessarily be on food—you may have a ravenous sexual appetite. Consider whether there is an imbalance in your life that needs redressing. Alternatively, perhaps you are over-indulging in feelings of self-pity or are greedy for material things. You may need to set limits upon your desires.

Mystical Meaning All is well as long as you enjoy the food. If the food tastes bad or you are refused food, then you will soon experience disappointments.

FEATHER

Psychological Meaning Feathers can represent a gift that expresses your desire to show warmth and tenderness to someone close to you. A feather floating in the air may show your desire to ascend to higher spiritual knowledge or intellectual ambition. The lightness of a feather also implies lightheartedness and enjoyment of the good things in life. You may benefit if you surrender for a while to the benevolent winds of fortune. Go with the flow.

Mystical Meaning Many cultures, such as the Incas and Native Americans, used feathered headdresses to represent spiritual authority and wisdom.

FENCE

Psychological Meaning You may feel that there are barriers in your way. You feel fenced in and restricted in what you can do or can express. Perhaps your relationship is unsatisfactory because you feel that your partner does not allow you to be the person you really are. Similarly, you may feel that your job or circumstances are restrictive to your personal growth. It's time to pull down these fences and be yourself.

Mystical Meaning A fence is an obstacle and is therefore interpreted by the ancient dream seers as difficulties ahead.

FIELDS

Psychological Meaning The openness of a field may express your desire to be free. A field is also a fertile place and may therefore symbolize personal growth. The earth can symbolize the mother, which in turn represents the instinctive levels of your being, from which this growth may come. Alternatively, the dream may simply represent your love of and desire to be with nature. In times of trouble, a short break spent with nature can be very therapeutic. Many of society's ills are caused by losing touch with nature's restorative and nurturing powers.

Mystical Meaning The Gypsies believe that to dream of a field means a great deal of hard work ahead. A field of weeds will have little reward, but if it is full of clover you will soon make wealthy friends.

FIGHTING (*see* War)

FILM

Psychological Meaning What you watched on TV or saw at the cinema before going to bed can influence your dreams. You may have unconsciously felt an empathy for something you saw. To dream of watching a film may demonstrate that you are contemplating your thoughts in an unattached way. You are able to view yourself and your life without becoming emotionally involved.

Mystical Meaning Medieval sources of course do not list this one, but more modern superstitions say that to dream of handling film signifies that you will receive a gratifying gift.

FINGERS

Psychological Meaning If you subscribe to Freud's theories, then fingers are clearly phallic symbols. Alternatively, they may represent dexterity or its opposite, ineptitude, and being "all thumbs." A finger pointing at you can imply self-blame. Alternatively, it may point to indicate a direction. In this case, your dream may be solving problems for you and may be suggesting what you should do. Consider what aspect of yourself or your situation the dream has pointed out and give it your attention.

Mystical Meaning It is fortunate to dream of cutting your finger, but only if it bleeds. And if you dream of having an extra finger, you will receive an inheritance.

FIRE

Psychological Meaning Fire destroys, but it also cleanses and purifies. It can illuminate, but it also causes pain. Its energy is a potent symbol of eternal life or eternal damnation. Fire is a powerful yet ambivalent dream symbol.

In dreams, it can signal a new beginning, spiritual illumination, sexual passion, or disruptive emotions, such as the flames of passion or envy. For example, to dream of a house burning down or a forest fire warns that you are consumed by passion. Consider whether your emotions are getting out of control and whether you need to calm the flames. Are you being a hothead? Do you have a fiery temper? Be careful or your burning passion may spark a flaming argument!

Fire can also be a symbol of security. To dream of a cozy fire in the hearth shows that you are comfortable with your circumstances and at ease with your life. Freud said that fire was a symbol of the libido (the passions), and to dream of poking a fire represented arousing sexual passion.

Mystical Meaning Jung said that fire represents the process of psychological transformation. Just as the alchemists used fire to transform base metal into gold, so the symbol fire is the trigger for the inner transformation. It purges the decay of the past, yet gives light and spiritual truth. It is the eternal flame in the temple of the soul. It is from the fire that the phoenix of hope arises.

FISH

Psychological Meaning Fish can represent insights into the unconscious. (The unconscious is represented by the sea.) Jung said that fish are often symbols used by the dream to describe psychic happenings or experiences that suddenly dart out of the unconscious and have a frightening or redeeming effect. Fish caught in a net and brought to the surface may represent insights emerging into the light of consciousness. Fish are also a common symbol of fertility. Your dream may be indicating that you are experiencing a period of personal growth. Fish are a product of the emotions and intuition, as opposed to the materialistic, earthbound approach to life.

Mystical Meaning A fish is a symbol for Christ. Fish have also been used as a symbol by many other religions to represent divinity. They represent the spiritual abundance that feeds everyone. Your dream may be a mystical insight into your divine potential.

FLOATING

Psychological Meaning In order to float you have to relax and accept the support of the water. In psychological terms, this means that you have accepted the feminine side of your psyche and are carried forward by it. Floating implies acceptance; you have let go of your problems, worries, and restrictions and can now enjoy just being yourself. Go with the flow.

Mystical Meaning To dream of floating means tremendous success will come your way, but if you struggle to stay afloat there will be delays.

FLOOD

Psychological Meaning Water symbolizes the emotional side of the unconscious. To dream of a flood or of being swept away by water indicates that you feel emotionally overwhelmed. These dreams also hint at baptism and rebirth. The fertile, nourishing effect of floodwater may be implied. This dream could therefore represent the start of a new phase of life and of renewed personal growth.

Mystical Meaning The story of Noah's ark, the *Epic of Gilgamesh*, and other myths about floods represent a purging that prepares the way for something better. Everything in your life has been swept away so that you may start anew.

FLOWER (SEE ALSO MANDALA)

Psychological Meaning A flower is a symbol of the true spiritual self. Its symmetry and perfection show how beautiful you really are.

Mystical Meaning At first the Buddha felt that enlightenment was impossible to convey to the

FLYING

world. Then he saw a pond of lotus flowers at different stages of unfolding. He understood that all people are at different stages of spiritual development. Like the flowers, some remain in the mud of desire, but others raise themselves and gradually open to the light. Inspired by what he saw, the Buddha began his mission.

Common Dream

FLYING

I dreamed I could fly in the air, rose above the town below, and flew high into the night sky. It felt wonderful. I had no fear and could float gently down to earth whenever I wanted.—Charles N., New York

Psychological Meaning To dream of flying is usually a pleasant experience accompanied by a sense of exhilaration and freedom. It usually feels completely natural, something you've always known how to do. Rarely is the dream accompanied by a fear of heights or of falling. Flying may symbolize liberation from something that has been troubling you. The obstructions and shackles that have held you down have been released, and you can now experience the same sense of freedom seen in the birds that soar in the sky. The sky may symbolize consciousness and spirituality, so to dream of flying can represent the expansion of your awareness and the unfolding of your higher self. (To Freud, flying dreams represented sexual release.)

Nevertheless, flying also has its perils. The ancient Greek myth of Icarus warns against flying too high. Your dream may show that you are being overly ambitious.

ASK YOURSELF

1. *What is it I am being released from?* Think about the things that have been troubling you of late. Perhaps the difficulty or emotional problem that has grounded you for so long is not as bad as you thought. Sometimes it is important to tread the paths of life lightly. Let the freedom, gentleness, and carefree feeling of the dream be expressed in your behavior.

2. *Do I feel anxiety or fear?* You may thrill at the feeling of risk that your dream gives you. If so, you

may want to take more risks in your life, for example, with your work or a relationship. If you feel trepidation and alarm, you may be over-reaching yourself and may need to get a firmer footing in your life. Your dreams and ambitions may be too grandiose and not in accord with what you can realistically expect to achieve.

Mystical Meaning In ancient times, a person who dreamed of flying was considered to have entered the realm of the immortal gods. Native Americans, Babylonians, Hindus, Tibetan Buddhists, and many others claim that all people have a light body that can leave the physical body during sleep. The light body can travel great distances and even into other dimensions that mystics call the astral planes. Here it is possible to talk to friends who also travel the dimensions, communicate with the people of the spirit world, or learn from the advanced souls once called gods and angels. Many scientists believe that there is empirical proof that out-of-body travel is possible. For example, Dr Michael Sabom in *Recollections of Death* published six in-depth descriptions by patients of their surgical operations as purportedly viewed by them while out of the body. He substantiated their claims by comparing their reports with the surgeon's notes and other eyewitness testimony.

FOG (SEE ALSO BLIND AND CLOUDS)

Psychological Meaning You are not seeing things as they really are. You may be disoriented in waking life and have lost your sense of direction. It's time to finish with this foggy thinking. Be clear about what you want and what direction you want your life to take. Decisiveness will improve your inner clarity.

Mystical Meaning If the fog is thick, this is a very bad omen, say the dream oracles, but if you dream of it clearing, you will have great success.

FOOD (SEE ALSO EATING)

Psychological Meaning Food represents the qualities you take into yourself, and for Sigmund Freud it symbolized sexuality (see Eating). The different types of food you dream about can symbolize a variety of things. Fruit can symbolize sensuality, but it can also represent receiving rewards or abundance. To dream of bitter fruits such as lemons may indicate that you feel bitter-

FOOD

ness about a situation or person influencing your life. Are you the one with the sour attitude? Milk can symbolize human kindness; sugar, sweet words; and frozen food may indicate that you have frozen emotions. There are thousands of possible qualities symbolized by food. You will need to examine what your personal associations are with the food featured in your dream. For example, Freud considered that chocolate or any luxurious food represented self-reward. Do you get a feeling of guilt when you look at a cake? And could it therefore represent guilt in your dreams?

Mystical Meaning Since the times of the Ancient Greeks to dream of food was interpreted in sexual terms. Peaches and other succulent fruits stood for lasciviousness, while others, such as pomegranates, symbolized fertility. It was an apple the caused Adam and Eve to be booted out of the Garden of Eden. Food such as bread symbolized a more restrained, fertility-orientated sexuality, and many cultures believe that if you eat meat you will take on the spiritual qualities of that particular animal.

FOOT

Psychological Meaning Your dream may be telling you to be practical and sensible. "Keep your feet squarely on the ground," says your unconscious. Alternatively, you may be reconsidering your direction in life or questioning what your life is based on. For a Christian, dreaming of washing feet is a symbol of forgiveness. In India, the feet of the guru are considered the holiest part of the body and a symbol of the divine.

Mystical Meaning In China they say: "All great journeys begin with a single step." Your dream may be advising you to move forward one step at a time.

FOREIGN COUNTRIES

Psychological Meaning To dream of being in foreign countries means that you are experiencing something unfamiliar in your waking life. For example, you may have changed your job or may be behaving in ways that are different from your usual routine. If the surroundings make you feel lost or anxious, your dream may be telling you that you are not yet ready to leave your old way of life behind. You are not yet prepared to deal with a new set of circumstances that are influencing your life. However, if you feel excitement at discovering something new, your dream is reflecting your pleasure at finding new openings in your waking life. Now is the time to take advantage of new opportunities that are presenting themselves to you.

Mystical Meaning If you have patience, your wishes will come true.

FOREIGNER

Psychological Meaning A foreigner may represent a part of the psyche that is unfamiliar to you. You may be neglecting important feelings or talents that you need to get acquainted with.

Mystical Meaning Superstition tells that a friendly foreigner predicts good luck.

FOREST

Psychological Meaning The forest is often a symbol of the unconscious. Its animals and birds can be symbols for the instincts and emotions. To dream of trying to find your way through a dark forest may represent that you are searching for a breakthrough in your waking life.

Mystical Meaning Many fairy tales such as *Hansel and Gretel* and *Snow White* are set in the forest. Just like dreams, these stories represent exploring the world of the unconscious mind.

FAMOUS DREAMER

Adolf Hitler
Nazi dictator

During the First World War, 28-year-old Adolf Hitler was a corporal in the German Infantry fighting in the trenches on the French front. One night, he dreamed of being buried beneath an avalanche of earth and molten iron. He could feel the terrible pain of being fatally wounded. He woke up and felt compelled to leave the trench. As soon as he was clear of the dugout, he heard a loud explosion behind him. The trench he had been sleeping in only moments before was now a smoldering pile of dirt, hot metal, and blood. This event convinced Hitler he was invincible and destined for greatness.

FOUNTAIN (SEE ALSO MANDALA AND WATER)

Psychological Meaning A fountain is a symbol of the life force. It may represent the source of your vitality, the spiritual center from which you draw your inspiration and joy. Fountains that are symmetrical or are built upon a circular pool are mandalas symbolizing the unity of the self.

Mystical Meaning Predicts a happy, fulfilled period ahead, but if the fountain runs dry there will be problems.

FRAUD

Psychological Meaning You may feel that you have been cheated of the worldly success that you rightly deserve. Alternatively, it may be you who are the fraud by not expressing your true sentiments. Or perhaps you are simply taking advantage of people in your waking life. Honesty is your best policy.

Mystical Meaning To dream of unmasking a fraud or of catching a thief promises good fortune.

FRIEND

can represent your shadow self—the aspects of your personality that you have rejected. However, the shadow self in this dream is not portrayed as something sinister or threatening. You may be prepared to integrate this neglected part of yourself and restore inner harmony.

Mystical Meaning To dream that you have a friend who is always true is a promise of good news. If you dream that a friend is in trouble there will be worrying news.

FRUIT (SEE FOOD)

FRUSTRATION

Psychological Meaning If you dream of missing a train, being unable to read an important message, searching in vain for something, or failing to convince someone of the truth of an argument, your dream is expressing deep-set frustrations. You may be concerned that your life is not going in the direction you want, or may feel a repressed anger at the stubbornness of the people in your life. It is important that you discover why you feel so frustrated so that you can deal more effectively with its causes.

Mystical Meaning Dream superstition takes frustrations to mean the opposite—all your plans will succeed.

FUNERAL (SEE ALSO DEATH)

Psychological Meaning Don't take this one too literally. The person being buried may represent an aspect of yourself you are trying to repress. Is there something you want removed from your life? Perhaps you have feelings, desires, or thoughts that scare you. You may be worrying too much about your health, or perhaps you want to bury the past. The only constant in life is change. The past is dead and buried, so embrace the present and look forward to the future.

Who is being buried? Do you feel resentment toward this person, or does the person symbolize something happening in your life or something about yourself? If you are being buried in the dream, you may have a fear about being overwhelmed by your emotional troubles or by unconscious forces. First, get in touch with these hidden feelings and find out what they are. What happened recently (or a long time ago) to give rise to these emotions? Don't keep burying them. Start by examining them, then accept them, and finally start to control them. The problems you try to bury are probably not as bad as you think.

Mystical Meaning Occasionally dreams of funerals do foretell the future. For example, Abraham Lincoln dreamed of his own death just days before he was assassinated. He saw his own shrouded corpse laid in state in a room of the White House. However, in the vast majority of cases, dreams of funerals are a metaphor for your own state of mind.

FUTURE

Psychological Meaning To dream of being in the future may represent the way you hope or fear things will turn out. Your dream may be saying, "If you carry on behaving the way you are, this is the situation you're likely to find yourself in." However, your dream may not necessarily be a premonition of actual events to come.

Mystical Meaning J. W. Dunne in his famous book *An Experiment with Time* proposed that dreams can tell of future events and cited many examples from his dream diaries. However, it is wise not to take these dreams too literally, for the unconscious can distort the information it receives. For example, Dunne dreamed of being *killed* by a bull. In the next few days he was *chased* by a bull but certainly not killed.

GAG

Psychological Meaning The dream may be saying that you cannot express the way you really feel about an issue. There are important things that need saying but you don't know how to say them. Alternatively, the dream may be saying the opposite. Your unconscious may be warning you to keep quiet.

Mystical Meaning An obstacle dream that suggests difficulties with communications may lead to misunderstanding. Beware of gossip.

GAMBLING

Psychological Meaning You may be involved in some kind of risk-taking in waking life. Weigh the odds and decide which option is the best. Occasionally, I have interviewed people who have dreamed of a winning horse or a run of numbers that wins a prize. However, I have also heard from many more people who have placed bets because of a dream and then lost! Don't be reckless if you bet.

Mystical Meaning Superstition says to reverse this dream. To dream of winning brings a loss, but to dream of losing brings a gain.

GARBAGE

Psychological Meaning This often symbolizes the unwanted traits, attitudes, fears, or memories that you want to discard. It may also symbolize a duty or responsibility that you want nothing to do with. Perhaps you feel you have now disposed of the junk in your life that has been preventing you from progressing. If the garbage is rotten, it implies that these difficulties have been with you for a long time.

Mystical Meaning Superstition says that dreaming of garbage means your wildest dreams will come true.

GARDEN

Psychological Meaning A garden is a promising dream symbol that may show inner growth and stability. Sometimes dream gardens are symmetrical with a central point. This mandala symbol represents the inner wholeness of your true self. Pools, water, and fountains show the pure spiritual energies that constitute your nature. This dream may indicate inner healing after a period of discord and unease.

Mystical Meaning Some sources claim that to dream of a garden foretells a marriage to a very beautiful woman or a handsome man.

GATE

Psychological Meaning Walking through a gateway may represent moving into a new phase of life. New opportunities may await you.

Mystical Meaning An open gate represents changes for the better, but a closed gate means problems ahead.

GHOST

Psychological Meaning The shadowy ghosts of your dream represent those aspects of yourself that you fear. But it is fear itself that makes them frightening. Expose these dark pursuing forces to the light of day and you will discover that it is only your own fear that turns them into nightmares. You must realize that many different energies make up your psyche. Accept them all as valid parts of yourself. Your dream may also reflect your own fears about death and dying. For Freud a ghost was a symbol of the mother.

Mystical Meaning In most cases ghosts are representations of the dark forces within yourself that you have not accepted. However, as a medium I have spoken to many people who claim to have met the dead in their dreams. In some cases, the spirit gave evidence that proved it to be the real spirit of someone from the next world. Only spirits that truly care for you can communicate in this way.

GIANT

Psychological Meaning Giants can represent awe-inspiring powers that are dominating you or forcing you to take notice of them. Mythological giants are often connected with sex, and the club they often carry is considered by many psychologists to be a phallic symbol. For a man, to dream of a giant can indicate that sexual needs are disproportionate to the opportunities to gratify them. For a woman, to dream of a giant may indicate guilt or fear regarding sex. To adults a giant may be a recollection of childhood, when all adults towered above us. They may represent a protective or feared father figure.

GATE

Mystical Meaning To dream of a giant is a lucky omen that predicts commercial success.

GIFT

Psychological Meaning This dream shows how you interact with other people. If you receive many gifts, it may show that others hold you in esteem. If you are the giver, it may show that you desire to be generous to others. You may want to express your feelings or have something awkward to say that has to be carefully packaged. Does it show the way you disguise the things you say and do? What's inside the box may represent your true motives. Are they honorable?

Mystical Meaning To dream of being given a gift brings misfortune, but to dream of giving a gift means a new enterprise.

GOD

Psychological Meaning Your dream may be a truly spiritual dream. Sometimes the unconscious uses symbolism from ancient traditions to express your feelings about divinity. Put aside your material concerns and focus on higher things. It was a wise man who wrote "In God We Trust" on United States dollar bills. Goddesses and gods can also represent the anima and animus or can be symbols for the mother and father.

Mystical Meaning Most old dream books avoid this one because they were written in less tolerant times. To dream of the Christian God means you will achieve peace, but to dream of graven images signifies sexual pleasure.

GOLD

Psychological Meaning Precious gold may symbolize those aspects of your true self that you hold dear. It can represent spiritual achievement and self-realization. Associated with the sun, it may also represent life and renewal.

Mystical Meaning For the alchemists, gold represented the spiritual treasure that was gained by transforming the spirit. In mythology, it appears as the spiritual prize that is gained once the dragons and monsters of ignorance are overcome.

GOVERNMENT

Psychological Meaning A government may represent the forces within your psyche that have most power. Are you governed by qualities such as greed, lust, and jealousy, or love, acceptance, and honesty? What factors are in charge of your life? Dreaming about government may also reflect your views about society at large and about the way you organize your life.

Mystical Meaning To dream about holding a position of power within government indicates a period of uncertainty ahead.

GRANDPARENTS

Psychological Meaning Grandparents are usually seen by children to be more sympathetic figures than parents. Parents have to be obeyed, but a grandparent's advice is listened to and voluntarily applied. In dreams, they can represent wisdom that has stood the test of time. This wisdom may be the superior knowledge of the unconscious.

Mystical Meaning Even the wackiest of dream books agree that grandparents are a symbol of wisdom and security.

GRAVE

Psychological Meaning Something within you has died. You must discover what it is and why it has been returned to the unconscious, here symbolized by the earth. Alternatively, the grave may be a pun, suggesting that you are facing a "grave situation," or it could simply be a reflection of your own thoughts about death and mortality.

Mystical Meaning Superstitions say that this dream means you will experience a loss but not necessarily a death. Some superstitions say the dream foretells news of a marriage.

GREEN (SEE COLORS)

GUEST

Psychological Meaning A guest may represent a previously unconscious aspect of yourself that you have invited to become part of your conscious life. Similarly, a guest may represent new challenges and interests. If you are the guest, the dream may draw your attention to circumstances in your life that are temporary. Guests don't usually stay forever, they come, are entertained, and then they go.

Mystical Meaning The *I Ching* says: "When a man is a stranger, he should not be gruff or over-

GURU

bearing....He must be cautious and reserved; in this way he protects himself from evil. If he is obliging toward others, he wins success." Perhaps your dream gives similar advice.

GUN

Psychological Meaning When Mae West said in the film *My Little Chickadee* "Is that a gun in your pocket or are you just pleased to see me?" she was talking pure Freud. In dreams guns represent aggressive sexuality. If you dream of killing someone with a gun, it may represent your desire to kill off part of yourself. If it's an animal you kill, it may show that you repress your instincts. If it's you being shot, you may feel that in waking life you are being victimized in some way.

Mystical Meaning If you hear guns in a dream, expect a quarrel with a neighbor.

GURU

Psychological Meaning The guru may represent your own higher self and the innate wisdom within you. He may take a religious form such as Buddha, Shiva, or a saint. This inner guide may also appear as an old bearded man, a priest, prophet, magician, or king. In its feminine manifestation, it may appear as the Earth Mother or a goddess. For example, the Virgin Mary appearing within dreams is a symbol of supreme compassion and selfless love; your inner guide that teaches through grace rather than power. Carl Jung called these figures "mana personalities." (Mana denotes the mysterious powers associated with the gods, or superhuman knowledge.) Because of the awe-inspiring knowledge and insight these people represent, they may sometimes appear as frightening or domineering figures. Dreams of this nature indicate that an extremely important spiritual aspect of your life is opening.

Mystical Meaning Some spiritual traditions, such as those of the Tibetan Buddhists, Hindus, and Native Americans, believe that the inner teacher is a real person who communicates to the dreamer via another realm of existence. The teacher may come from this world or from the realms of spirit. I am a follower of the Indian guru Sathya Sai Baba, whom I believe has spoken to me directly through my dreams. To some of my friends he has confirmed this, by describing the content and repeating the exact words said by him in their dreams!

GYPSY

Psychological Meaning The Gypsies are a mysterious people surrounded by legends and occult stories and may therefore represent your shadow—the undiscovered part of yourself. Alternatively, the dream may be suggesting that you look to the future. What will your circumstances be like in years to come if you continue as you are?

Mystical Meaning As Gypsies are associated with prophecy, your dream may be giving you real clues to future events. Gypsies are associated with good luck, so destiny may smile upon you yet.

HAIR

Psychological Meaning Hair often symbolizes vanity. Long hair may signify virility or male sexuality. Dreams of going bald may indicate fears about loss of self-esteem or, according to Freud, fear of castration and impotency. Dreams about losing hair can also express worries about getting older. Similarly, a strong beard can stand for vitality, while a white one can signify age or wisdom. To dream of having your hair cut may indicate that you are, like Samson, experiencing a loss of strength. You may feel that someone is trying to censor you. To shave off the hair on the head symbolizes renunciation of the earthly life in order to seek spiritual truth. If your hair is being styled or set, then your dream is highlighting your worries about your self-image. Hair blown by the wind or flowing free indicates you may need the freedom to express uninhibited feelings. You want to "let your hair down" and "hang loose."

Mystical Meaning Cutting of hair can represent conformity. In the past, it was commonplace to cut the hair of convicts, soldiers, and schoolboys. When the Beatles grew long hair in the 60s, it was an unconscious symbol that expressed the rebellion of a generation.

HALL (SEE ALSO BUILDINGS)

Psychological Meaning A hall is the center from which you can access the whole house. To dream of entering a hall may therefore represent the beginning of your adventure in self-exploration.

Mystical Meaning To dream of a long hallway predicts a period of worry ahead.

HAMMER

Psychological Meaning A Freudian interpretation of hammering a nail is that it is a symbol for the sexual act. A hammer, therefore, is a powerful male symbol of virility, power, and strength. Alternatively, it may also represent the way you are dealing with your situation at the moment. Are you being too forceful? On the other hand, perhaps you are trying to "hammer the message home."

Mystical Meaning Thursday gets its name from the Teutonic god Thor, the son of Odin, who controlled the weather and crops. He possessed a magical hammer that would return to his hand after he had thrown it. In this instance, the hammer represents divine power and spiritual strength.

HANDS

Psychological Meaning Hands can represent dexterity, artistic ability, or psychological skills. You also use them to express yourself and as extensions of your personality. A fist may represent anger or passion, folded hands can represent acceptance, joined hands can represent affection, and an upheld hand symbolizes a blessing. Consider the gesture of the hands in your dream, for it reveals the nature of the sentiments you are trying to express.

Mystical Meaning If you dream of the palm, you may be thinking about the future. Palmistry claims that the shape, lines, and mounts of the palm reveal your destiny. Your dream may be revealing a *potential* future scenario based upon your current circumstances. Fortunately you have free will, so positive actions taken now will influence the shape of things to come for the better.

HARBOR

Psychological Meaning A harbor is a sanctuary from the stormy seas. Similarly, your dream shows that you have found a safe haven where you can wait until the storms pass. For the time being, seek refuge in the familiar and thereby prepare yourself for the challenges ahead. Use this period of security to grow in strength.

Mystical Meaning Superstition claims that to dream of entering a harbor predicts a period of security ahead, but dream of leaving one and you'll break a friendship.

HARE

Psychological Meaning The hare can be a symbol of the trickster who effects transformation. It is both a messenger from the unconscious and the weak but cunning inferior function at the threshold between consciousness and unconsciousness. It can represent some personal characteristic such as rashness or shallow cleverness.

Mystical Meaning Hares were always considered unlucky because it was believed that they were sometimes witches in disguise. It was also believed that if a pregnant woman saw one, her child would be born with a harelip. However,

HANDS

some dream oracles say that to dream of a hare approaching you brings good luck.

HAT

Psychological Meaning Freud believed that hats (and gloves) represent the female genitalia because they enclose a part of the body. A hat may also represent the role you play in life. Changing hats may denote a change of attitude or direction. You may be thinking about taking on new work responsibilities or even changing your job. The type of hat is also significant: a top hat may indicate your desire for wealth; a baseball hat may represent your desire to be more athletic or younger; and a straw hat may show that you desire to adopt a more natural, carefree attitude.

Mystical Meaning Predecessors of Freud believed that if a woman dreamed of wearing a man's hat, she secretly desired to have sex with the owner. If you dream of losing your hat, yous will soon be married.

HEAD

Psychological Meaning A head may symbolize rationality and the intellect. It is the conscious self. There may also be puns in the dream such as "keeping ahead of the game" or "facing your situation head-on." In addition, the dream may be a metaphor to express what is going on in your head at the moment.

Mystical Meaning It is a sign of good news if you dream that your head is very large, say the seers of old.

HEART

Psychological Meaning The heart represents the center of emotional life. It is an archetypal symbol for love that has been with humanity from time immemorial. Your dream is describing your emotional life and the way that you are currently dealing with your feelings. If the heart is damaged, being operated on, or wounded, then you may be experiencing an emotional hurt of some kind. Examine the rest of the dream's content to see if it reveals ways to repair the emotional damage that you feel. Alternatively, if the heart is pictured in a more positive setting, then your dream is saying that you feel good about your emotion-

al life. Dare you admit that you may have fallen in love?

Mystical Meaning In India, the heart is a symbol of *prema*—divine love. It also represents innermost motivations. My guru, Sathya Sai Baba, tells us to remember to observe ourselves every time we look at our watch. "WATCH: Watch your *Words*, *Actions*, *Thoughts*, *Character*, and *Heart*."

HEAVEN

Psychological Meaning To dream of a heavenly paradise may represent your desire to find perfect happiness. You may be trying to escape from what you perceive to be a banal and depressing life. Your dream gives you a welcome break from reality and serves to restore your feelings of optimism and hope. You desire to achieve the inner balance and wholeness that is your spiritual destiny.

Mystical Meaning I have on file many cases of people who have been taken in a dream to the afterlife. Here they have met their dead loved ones. The lucidity of the dreams suggests that these dreamers may be experiencing another level of reality. I believe that, in some rare cases, the dreamer is really communicating with the dead.

HEDGE

Psychological Meaning This dream may represent the restrictions and obstacles you believe are inhibiting your progress. The restrictions that you intend to overcome may be psychological or material. If you dream of cutting a hedge, it may suggest that you have accepted an immovable obstacle and are making the best of a bad situation.

Mystical Meaning To dream of cutting a hedge means that good luck is on its way.

HELL

Psychological Meaning You may have many inner fears and repressed guilty feelings that are forcing themselves into your awareness. Take it easy on yourself and stop punishing yourself. Once you have passed through this period of inner turmoil, you will emerge as a new and better person. Be gentle and accept yourself for the person you are. It is important that you now begin to tame the repressed contents of the unconscious and transform them into something positive.

Mystical Meaning The old dream dictionaries also say that this dream arises from inner strife. However, they add that it foretells improvements in business.

HERO/HEROINE (SEE ALSO ANIMA/ANIMUS)

Psychological Meaning Whether it be Gilgamesh, Hercules, or Superman, the hero figure represents the conscious part of yourself that bravely embarks on a journey into the darkness of the unconscious to challenge its wild powers. In most myths and stories, the hero ventures into strange lands and fights monsters in order to take possession of a great treasure or win the hand of a beautiful maiden. These are symbols of the rewards you gain by probing the unconscious mind. By taming its primitive forces and using them for creative ends, you achieve psychological integration and wholeness. For a woman, a male heroic figure may represent the masculine side of herself. Similarly, if a man dreams of rescuing a maiden, it may show that he has discovered the feminine side of his own nature.

Heroic dreams awaken you to your inner strengths and weaknesses—knowledge essential for the development of a healthy personality. Although these dreams generally occur during adolescence, they can also reappear at any age. As you would expect, males tend to have more hero dreams than women do, but this is changing as women take on roles that are more assertive.

Mystical Meaning Some dream sources claim that to dream of a famous heroic figure means that someone who once disliked you will now fall in love with you.

HILL

Psychological Meaning A hill may represent an obstacle that you have to overcome in waking life. If the journey is arduous, you may be attempting something beyond your strength. However, if the journey is easy, you may now have the inner resources you need to complete your task. Move forward one step at a time and be confident.

Mystical Meaning In this case, the superstitious interpretation is the same as the psychological one. A Freudian psychologist might add that hills represent a woman's breasts—probably your mother's.

HIVE

Psychological Meaning This dream may represent your lifestyle. You are probably extremely active and working very hard at the moment. And just like the busy bees, you need to be well organized. If you dream of something upsetting the order of the hive, this represents the factors that are disrupting the smooth running of your waking-life activities.

Mystical Meaning In rural superstition, bees were always considered to be wise creatures with a special knowledge of the future. Dreams that include bees or hives may hold clues to future events.

HOLE

Psychological Meaning To a Freudian psychologist, a hole represents the vagina or womb. Your dream may therefore be about sexual issues. It may also suggest that you feel hollow and empty within. Could it be that you have indulged so much in feelings of depression that it's as if you dug yourself into a hole that you can't get out of? You may need to introduce new interests into your life in order to restore your feeling of self-worth and fulfillment. To dream of holes in clothes may indicate that you are worried about your self-image.

Mystical Meaning To dream of crawling into a hole augurs badly. You will befriend seedy and unreliable people.

HOLIDAY (SEE VACATION)

HOME

Psychological Meaning This dream may be about your need for security. You may feel that your situation is better now. Do you feel at home in your job? Is your environment homely? Perhaps you feel that after a period of struggle you are now on home ground? Your dream may also include references to your own childhood or, if you are single, thoughts about starting a family of your own.

Mystical Meaning The nomadic Gypsies claim that to dream of being forced to leave your home indicates that a favorable opportunity awaits you.

HONEY

Psychological Meaning Honey represents sweetness and feelings that bring you happiness, such as love, peace, and joy. It is the spirit or life force that sustains you. In the Far East, lies are sometimes called "poisoned honey."

Mystical Meaning Honey is the food of the gods, so this dream may be showing your desire to attain divine consciousness.

HORSE

Psychological Meaning Wild forces that have been tamed are symbolized by the horse. Horses are also a symbol of sexuality and were considered by Freud to represent the terrifying aspect of the father. To dream of riding an out-of-control horse may indicate that you are being carried away by your passions, whereas a tightly tethered horse may show that you inhibit these natural feelings. If you fear the horses in your dream, then you may fear your own instinctive nature (literally a "night mare"). In short, horses represent the wild energies of the psyche that need to be both bridled and respected.

Mystical Meaning In some myths and fairy tales, horses speak. In dreams, this represents the voice of your unconscious—a message from your innermost self. In Greek myth, horses were associated with Hades, the underworld, and death. However, dream prophecy says that to dream of horses indicates that you will receive news from a

distance. And it is extremely lucky to dream of a horse being shod.

HOSPITAL

Psychological Meaning A hospital is a place of healing. Your dream may offer you cures to improve your psychological or physical health. Observe in which department your dream is set; it may give you important clues to the nature of your problem. You may need some rest or may be trying to recover from a psychological wound that requires inner healing. Or perhaps the dream is a warning about your physical health? Does the dream offer a cure? Does it suggest a healthier behavior pattern or diet? They called Edgar Cayce "The Sleeping Prophet" because he would fall asleep and answer questions put to him about the health of people he had never met. He gave startlingly accurate diagnoses, and his revolutionary treatments and cures are still being used and researched today. Hidden within dreams are the keys to spiritual, psychological, and physical health.

Mystical Meaning The Ancient Greeks believed that dreams not only give a diagnosis of a person's health but also suggest cures. In particular this was affirmed by Hippocrates, who is considered the father of medicine. Student doctors still pledge the Hippocratic Oath. Tibetan medicine also takes note of a patient's dreams in order to uncover the spiritual cause of physical ills.

HOTEL

Psychological Meaning A hotel is an impermanent abode and in dreams represents a transition from one set of circumstances to another. Your dream may highlight a feeling of impermanence or perhaps a shift or loss of personal identity. It may indicate a change in a relationship or the price that has to be paid to sustain it.

Mystical Meaning If the hotel is luxurious, failure is predicted, but if it's a seedy old motel, you will soon experience good fortune.

HOUSE (SEE ALSO BUILDINGS)

Psychological Meaning A house represents your psychological condition. Specific rooms in the house detail what aspect of your psychological life the dream is highlighting. Attic: the intellect. Basement: the personal unconscious. Bathroom: base feelings, childhood thoughts, and cleanliness. Bedroom: the private self and sexuality. Den: work and efficiency. Library: intellectual life. Living room: your public image. Roof: an overview of yourself. Windows: the way to interact with the world.

Mystical Meaning Dream lore has many different interpretations for this dream. Here's the simplest: country house, tranquility ahead; building a house, you will be self-confident; new house, a busy social life; empty house, low income; moving house, worries about money.

HUNGER

Psychological Meaning You may simply feel hungry. However, from a symbolic perspective this dream can represent a craving for sex, power, wealth, or fame. Perhaps you feel a lack of satisfaction and feel that your potential is not being recognized. You may be hungry for affection or an opportunity.

Mystical Meaning Superstition says that the hungrier you are, the more destiny will smile upon you.

HUNT (SEE ALSO CHASE)

Psychological Meaning The hunt represents your pursuit of what you want. You may be hunting for a solution, or perhaps you desire to achieve wealth or status. Is the dream about sexual conquest? If the hunt involves killing an animal, you may be trying to repress or destroy an instinctive aspect of yourself.

Mystical Meaning Dream lore says hunting a hare indicates trouble ahead, while a fox predicts deceit by a friend. However, if you dream of hunting a deer you will win the heart of your sweetheart.

HUSBAND

Psychological Meaning This may simply be a dream about your relationship and your unconscious feelings about him. However, you may also be projecting other qualities into this dream image. He may sometimes represent your father or the male side of your own personality (animus)

Mystical Meaning Superstition says that there will be troubles ahead if you dream of being married when you're not.

ICE (SEE ALSO WATER)

Psychological Meaning Water can show the creative flow of feelings, but as ice it shows that feelings are petrified and progress is stopped. You may feel emotionally paralyzed, so pay more attention to your emotional life and become more attuned to your affections. Perhaps you feel that a situation requires you to "break the ice"? You need to experience warm, wholesome feelings expressed with sincerity. Love will melt your frozen heart.

Mystical Meaning If you are married, this dream predicts that you will be happy, but to dream of skating bodes disaster.

ILLNESS

Psychological Meaning This dream does not necessarily presage a waking illness but may represent uncleared bad feelings. You may not be able to cope with a situation and, like a child, may take illness as an easy way out. Perhaps the dream represents a form of self-punishment.

Mystical Meaning Superstitious people believe that dreams should be reversed. This dream therefore predicts a period of good health.

INCEST

Psychological Meaning If the dream relates to real-life events, consider seeking professional advice or counseling. For a man, to dream of incest with a daughter symbolically expresses a fear of secret erotic desires. Incest with a sister or brother can represent the union of masculine and feminine sides of the dreamer. For a man, to dream of incest with his mother represents the desire he may have had for her as a small boy (*see* Mother) and likewise a woman's dreams of incest with her father represent her infantile desires (*see* Father).

Mystical Meaning The subject was so taboo, ancient dream books made no comment about these dreams.

INFIDELITY

Psychological Meaning The dream may be wish-fulfillment. Perhaps you feel unsatisfied with your relationship and feel the need for a more exotic sexual life. It is the nature of biology

INTERNET

that both sexes are tempted to be adulterous. Erotic dreams about people other than your partner may sometimes act as a safety valve to release these powerful urges. Surveys indicate that the happiest people are those with a good partnership based on faithfulness and an extended circle of friends. If you dream that your partner is unfaithful, it may indicate that you are neglecting your partner's emotional needs.

Mystical Meaning Dream superstition says that this dream means the opposite. You and your partner will be faithful to each other.

INITIATION

Psychological Meaning These dreams usually represent the transition from one psychological stage to a higher one. For example, they may represent moving from childhood to adolescence, from youth to middle age, or from middle age to old age. It can also represent the shift of interest from worldly ambitions to spiritual aspirations.

Mystical Meaning In ancient times, rituals and initiations were used as a creative dramatization of the pattern and structure of the psyche and life.

INJECTION

Psychological Meaning Clearly, a syringe can be a phallic symbol, so your dream may be saying that you need to inject more enthusiasm into your sex life. Similarly, it may be telling you to inject more fun, determination, or enthusiasm into your life. Injections imply healing and protection, so this dream may be showing you ways to become more psychologically fit.

Mystical Meaning A dream interpretation from the 1930s says that dreaming of being injected means you will be free of enemies who are plotting against you.

INSECTS

Psychological Meaning Insects symbolize the irritating minor nagging of the unconscious or daily life. You may have many irritating small problems that need to be dealt with. In Franz Kafka's book *Metamorphosis* (1912), the terrified sleeper wakes up to discover he has been transformed into a bug. Kafka worked most of his life in office jobs that he hated. Symbolically this dream can represent how working life requires you to form a brittle shell that can eventually take over your personality completely. Here are a few of the symbolic meanings of common insects: Ants: your life may be too orderly; ants can represent social conformity. Bees: industry and work. Butterflies: the soul, spiritual transcendence. Flies: breakdown, putrefaction, and perhaps guilt. Ladybugs: happiness at work. Locusts: lack of psychological nourishment; your creativity is being destroyed. Wasps: Angry thoughts and feelings.

Mystical Meaning The ancient Egyptians worshiped the scarab beetle as a symbol of creation. In dreams, it can represent the soul. In some fairy tales, insects are called in when things have become impossibly muddled. For example, they may be asked to separate grain mixed with sand or to remove gold dust from grain. In dreams, they can represent precision and meticulous thinking.

INTERNET

Psychological Meaning Your dream may represent the need to communicate with a wider group of friends. What sites do you connect to in your dream? These represent the psychological qualities and needs that your unconscious draws your attention to. E-mail can represent messages from your unconscious.

Mystical Meaning Psychics believe that all life is interconnected by a mycelium of living energy. What happens in one place affects everywhere else. By tuning into this spiritual World Wide Web, it is possible to use clairvoyance to perceive events taking place on the other side of the world. (Remote viewing is a good example of this.) In dreams, it is sometimes possible to connect to this ethereal Internet of consciousness.

INVALID

Psychological Meaning If you dream of being an invalid you may feel that something has robbed you of your ability or self-confidence. You may feel that you are unable to act in the way you really want to. Perhaps you feel crippled by your own negative feelings or by the scorn of others? The word "invalid" may also be a pun. You may feel that something is not valid. Perhaps somebody is not revealing his or her true feelings, or a mode of behavior has become obsolete.

Mystical Meaning Success will come slowly.

INVISIBLE

Psychological Meaning You may feel that nobody is taking notice of you, that what is important to you is of no consequence to others. Alternatively, you may feel that you want to hide from reality, or the dream could be a metaphor for shyness.

Mystical Meaning In the Ancient Greek mythology, Perseus used a cloak of invisibility. In dreams this can represent the hidden spiritual strength that is needed when exploring the unconscious.

IRON

Psychological Meaning Iron can represent inner strength but also ruthlessness. It is a metal associated with the Earth and the inferior, whereas mercury and gold are associated with spirituality. A household iron may show your desire to create order in your life. You want to "iron out the wrinkles." It may also be a dream that expresses your concerns about your self-image. A hair curling iron may show the opposite, that you want to put a bit of bounce into your life.

Mystical Meaning To dream of iron augurs badly. It is said to be an omen of distress.

ISLAND

Psychological Meaning You may have a craving for solitude if you dream a desert island. Perhaps you are surrounded by too many problems and need to make a little space for yourself? The sea often symbolizes the unconscious mind, so your desire to remain on an island may suggest a wish to cling to the conscious ego instead of venturing into these unexplored parts of yourself. The sea is also a mother symbol and can, according to Freudian psychology, symbolize relations with your mother. If the island is engulfed by the sea, this can represent a fear of being overwhelmed by too strong a mother-attachment or by unconscious forces out of your control

Mystical Meaning Comfort and easy circumstances are predicted by the ancient dream oracles.

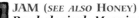

JAM (*SEE ALSO* HONEY)

Psychological Meaning There is an English saying: "Jam yesterday, jam tomorrow, but never jam today." This dream may represent your feeling that you keep missing the rewards of hard work and live forever on promises. Jam may represent the sweet things in life. Alternatively the dream may be a pun. Are you "in a jam" or a "sticky mess"? If your jam is covered in wasps you may feel that your security is threatened by people or events that threaten you.

Mystical Meaning If a woman dreams of making jam, she will be surrounded by appreciative friends.

JEALOUSY

Psychological Meaning These are probably feelings that you have carried forward from your waking life. Your dream may be revealing covetous feelings that you were previously unaware of. Similarly, you may have unconsciously recognized jealousy from your family, friends, or colleagues. Your dream may be warning you.

Mystical Meaning Dream oracles warn of narrow-minded people and the clandestine influence of enemies.

JEW

Psychological Meaning You may feel that you are being persecuted by prejudiced people if you dream of being Jewish. Alternatively, your dream may be telling you to be more tolerant toward others. You may associate Jews with borrowing or lending money and careful management of funds. If you are Jewish, this dream may be about your faith and about your relationship to members of your own community

Mystical Meaning To dream of a Jew indicates that you will prosper or win legal disputes. Yiddish proverbs are full of wisdom. One of my favorites says: "Do not worry about tomorrow; you do not even know what may happen to you today."

JEWELS (*SEE ALSO* TREASURE)

Psychological Meaning Jewels represent something you value within yourself or in other people. This may include a valued trait such as patience, creativity, assertiveness and so on, or it may represent core human values such as truth, non-violence, love, peace, and right conduct. Traditionally, gold and diamonds represent the incorruptible true self; rubies denote passion; emeralds, fertility; and sapphires, truth. **Mystical Meaning** Predicts good luck.

JOKE

Psychological Meaning Jokes are often funny because they disrupt your normal way of perceiving the world. Your unconscious may be trying to draw your attention to a serious issue that you need to consider. Even in dreams the truest things are often said in jest.
Mystical Meaning A funny joke told in a dream means that business will boom, but if it falls flat then so will your fortunes.

FAMOUS DREAMER

Mary Shelley
Author

In the summer of 1816, Mary Shelley and her husband, the famous poet Percy Bysshe Shelley, had been staying with friends at the Villa Deodati on the shores of Lake Geneva. They spent the evening telling ghost stories. Afterward, Percy suggested that each one of them write a horror story.

That night Mary Shelley had a terrifying dream. "My imagination, unbidden, possessed and guided me," she wrote, "gifting the successive images that arose in my mind with a vividness far beyond the usual bounds of reveries....I saw the pale student of unhallowed arts kneeling beside the thing he had put together— I saw the hideous phantasm of a man stretched out, and then, on the working of some powerful engine, show signs of life, and stir with an uneasy, half-vital motion."

When Mary Shelley awoke she immediately wrote down the nightmare. "What terrified me will terrify others; and I need only describe the specter which had haunted my midnight pillow."

Inspired by this nightmare, in 1818 she wrote her most famous book, Frankenstein: the Modern Prometheus.

JOURNEY (SEE ALSO ACCIDENTS, AIRPLANE, CAR, TRAIN)

Psychological Meaning The act of dreaming is a journey of discovery into the center of yourself. Consequently, there are many meanings associated with this dream theme. First, the dream may represent your journey through life. An open road suggests progress, but a rocky path may show that you feel your way is arduous. Lush scenery may show that you feel happy with your circumstances, but an arid desert may indicate loneliness or a lack of creativity. Sometimes the hard path is the right way forward, or you may want to establish a more comfortable, easygoing, pattern of behavior.

Are you aware of the destination and goal of your journey? Perhaps it is to discover your true self. You may feel that you tread on hallowed ground as you come closer to your own inner divinity. Sometimes the paths take you to strange lands or unfamiliar foreign countries. This can mean that your unconscious is inviting you to explore it. In mythology, a journey to the west can symbolize the journey to old age whereas an eastward journey can indicate rejuvenation. If towns feature in your dream, consider what they represent. For example, Paris may show that you have a romantic frame of mind, whereas cold Moscow may symbolize an emotional Cold War between you and your partner. You will also have many personal associations relating to places. Ask yourself what they represent and what feelings they represent.
Mystical Meaning The old-fashioned dream interpretations correspond to the modern meanings. For example, ease of travel or obstacles reflect the ease or difficulty you will find in the future. In addition, medieval mystics said that to dream of seeing cheerful friends starting out on a journey means that you will experience a very happy period ahead.

JUDGE

Psychological Meaning A judge may represent self-reproach or guilt. You may fear getting caught or having a secret plan revealed. Your dream may be helping you decide what to do, it is helping you make a judgment of your situation. Sometimes judges can represent society and the way it judges you. Freud believed that a judge was a personification of the super-ego—the standards of conventional morality that you assimi-

JUGGLING

lated from your parents and society. This aspect of yourself may censor your instinctive feelings and desires.

Mystical Meaning Your sharp tongue will make you a new friend.

JUGGLING

Psychological Meaning The dream illustrates that you are trying to keep all the elements of your life in order and in action. You are doing too much.

Mystical Meaning Superstition says that your indecision will lead to failure.

JUMPING

Psychological Meaning If you are jumping to orders, then your dream may be telling you to be more assertive. Stop obeying the will and whims of others. Be your own master and soon you'll dream of jumping for joy.

Mystical Meaning According to superstition, if you trip while jumping you will overcome difficulties and eventually gain success.

JUNGLE

Psychological Meaning A jungle is a symbol of the unconscious and its animals represent the untamed primitive instincts. Locked away in the collective unconscious are archaic memories of primordial times. Some dreams about jungles may be million-year-old memories passed on by distant ancestors. The French painter Henri Rousseau captured the wonderful mystery of these strange dreams in paintings such as his 1907 work, *La Charmeuse de Serpents*.

Mystical Meaning Problems ahead if you get lost, but they will clear if you dream of finding your way out.

 KEY

Psychological Meaning Clearly this can be a phallic symbol, and to dream of placing a key in a lock can represent sexual intercourse. Alternatively, the key may be a symbol for the solution to a problem. Your dreams may be showing you the way to unlock the door and to remove the psychological or material obstacles that block your progress.

Mystical Meaning To dream of finding a key is a symbol of good fortune, and a bunch of keys indicates profitable business dealings.

KILLING

Psychological Meaning If you murder someone in your dream, you are expressing your hatred or envy toward the person. Sometimes the person being killed can represent an aspect of your own nature that you hate. For example, if a man dreams of killing a woman, it may show that he rejects the feminine side of his nature. Similarly, if a woman dreams of killing a man, she may be rejecting her masculine side. To dream of killing animals indicates repression of your instinctive nature.

Mystical Meaning There will be arguments and you may have to make sacrifices, say the dream seers.

KING (SEE ALSO QUEEN)

Psychological Meaning A king can symbolize the self that sits on the throne of consciousness. He represents the dominant ruling power—the part of you that is in control. The king can also represent your father.

Mystical Meaning Carl Jung recognized alchemy as a system of symbolism representing the transformation of the lower self (base matter) into the divine (gold). The king is the human personification of the work. His appearance in dreams can have a number of important meanings: The king who is ill represents worn-out attitudes and sometimes the conflict between the conscious and unconscious. The decrepit king shows limited, ego-bound consciousness. If the king dissolves or returns to the mother, this shows the ego sinking back into unconsciousness. In the strange symbolism of alchemy, when a king gives birth to a hermaphrodite, it shows how the new, dominant self is born.

KISS

Psychological Meaning This could be a straightforward sexual dream. However, a kiss is also a symbol of love and affection, and so may represent those things you hold dear. Perhaps there are other connotations: the kiss of death, or the kiss of betrayal. The dream highlights the feelings that you have a closeness with at the moment.

Mystical Meaning The Gypsies believe that to dream of exchanging a kiss means that a quarrel will be over soon.

KITCHEN (SEE ALSO BUILDINGS)

Psychological Meaning In psychological terms, the food prepared in a kitchen is symbolic of the spiritual nourishment you give yourself.

Mystical Meaning If the kitchen is clean and tidy it is an auspicious dream that predicts harmony within the family.

KITE (SEE ALSO FLYING)

Psychological Meaning To dream of flying can symbolize your desire to be free of problems and to enjoy a more carefree and adventurous lifestyle. Similarly, kites symbolize the same connotations, except in a more controlled way. Just as a kite is tethered by a string, so you have not let go completely. It can also show that you desire to take control of your life. In England, a person who wants to take control of circumstances would be described as "wanting to fly his own kite." The expression often relates to self-employment or the process of setting up a business.

Mystical Meaning To dream of flying a kite denotes a great show of wealth, but if the kite crashes or the string breaks, expect financial troubles.

KNIFE

Psychological Meaning Most psychologists consider the knife or dagger a symbol of male sexuality. It can represent the penis in its ability to penetrate. It is also representative of masculinity and its associations with violence and aggression. You may be harboring a deep-seated destructive wish and may have repressed your feelings of anger. Is it you who carries the knife, or are you threatened by someone else? Identify with the possessor of the knife and discover if you are repressing angry feelings. The knife is also reminiscent of the "sword of truth" that cuts through falsity and ignorance or the will to cut away false desires.

Mystical Meaning They say that it is good luck to dream of a kitchen knife, but all other knives predict possible danger.

KNOCK

Psychological Meaning Your unconscious may be trying to attract your attention to something important you are unaware of at the moment.

Mystical Meaning To dream of someone knocking on a door indicates that soon fortune will smile on you.

KNOT

Psychological Meaning A knot may represent a problem that you're trying to untangle (a knotty problem). It can also represent the union of two people or the union of the male and female aspects of the psyche (i.e., tying the knot—a ritual that was an actual occurrence during Babylonian times, when threads from the couple's garments would be tied together).

Mystical Meaning Superstition has associated knots with problems. For example, at weddings the bridegroom should wear one of his shoes unlaced, to foil witches from untying his bride's virginity. Moreover, in Scotland it is believed that a corpse should not be put into a coffin with knots on any of its clothing or the spirit will never rest in peace. In dream superstitions, to dream knots means that you will meet with much to cause you anxiety.

LABORATORY

Psychological Meaning A laboratory may represent the transformation of the self (*see* Alchemy). It may also symbolize psychological experimentation and new ways of dealing with the world. You may be experimenting with ideas and perhaps even testing yourself. Could it be that you want to prove a point?

Mystical Meaning To dream of a laboratory is a warning of ill health, says superstition.

LADDER

Psychological Meaning A ladder may represent the different levels of consciousness between man and his divine self. It is a symbol of achieving personal wholeness. As a worldly symbol, climbing a ladder may represent progress such as achieving status, power, or an important goal. Descending a ladder may represent the opposite or an escape from your spiritual responsibilities.

Mystical Meaning The Biblical story of Jacob's ladder is a symbol for the communication between this world and the spiritual realm. Similarly, in Mesopotamia the Ziggurat was named "the ladder to heaven." In psychological terms this mystic symbolism can be understood as the communication between the true self and the ego. Consider this quote from Twitchell: "The higher one climbs on the spiritual ladder, the more he will grant others their own freedom and give less interference to another's state of consciousness."

LAKE

Psychological Meaning A lake may represent the unconscious mind. Water often makes a symbolic statement about your emotional state. If the lake is clear and still, it may represent your reserves of inner peace and spiritual energy. However, if the lake is disturbed in any way, you may have emotional trouble.

Mystical Meaning In Japanese Zen Buddhism the lake is a symbol of the mind. If its surface is moving you cannot see the moon's reflection. However, if the lake is allowed to be still, the moon appears. So too the mind must become still if it is to perceive enlightenment.

LAMB

Psychological Meaning Lambs may represent the part of you that is pure and innocent. It is the real you, unsullied by the troubles of this world.

Mystical Meaning The sacrificial lamb of God takes away the sins of the world. In a psychological sense, this represents a desire to find forgiveness.

LAMP

Psychological Meaning Light offers guidance and reassurance and is a symbol of the spirit. Similarly, the lamp is a positive symbol that may represent the hopes and inspiration that drive you on through dark times. If your lamp goes out, it may be a symbol that you are overwhelmed by the unconscious. You have lost your ability to find your own way.

Mystical Meaning The Hermit card from the Tarot pictures a wise old man carrying a lamp. Just like your dream, it advises you to carry your own spiritual light. It is a symbol of the wisdom that comes from free will and discrimination.

LEADING

Psychological Meaning If you dream of leading something, it shows you are taking control of factors in your life. What you are leading describes what you are taking control of. For example, if you dream of leading a dog, it may show that you are disciplining and controlling your sexual nature. If you are the one being led, consider what psychological factors you are following at the moment. Are you being led astray or toward something better?

Mystical Meaning Your dream may represent your desires. Eastern traditions teach that a person led by desire will never achieve happiness. Only by becoming the master of yourself and placing a "ceiling on desire" can you realize your innate divinity.

LECTURE

Psychological Meaning Your dream may be a continuation of your intellectual thinking and you are assimilating new knowledge that you learned during the day. However, the dream may be saying that you are becoming a bit of a bore by the way you lecture people in real life. You need to improve your communication skills. Don't be like Gladstone, a prime minister of Britain, about whom Queen Victoria complained: "[He] talks to me as if he is addressing a public meeting."

Mystical Meaning An odd British superstition claims that if you dream of giving a lecture about a poet, all your wishes will come true.

LEFT

Psychological Meaning The right hemisphere of the brain controls the left side of the body. This part of the brain is instinctive, artistic, and intuitive. The left side of the body therefore represents these qualities.

Mystical Meaning It was once believed that the Devil stood on the left, prompting a person to do wrong.

LEGS

Psychological Meaning Legs represent your ability to progress. If they are strong, it shows your self-confidence, but if they are weak, you may feel emotionally unsteady at the moment.

Mystical Meaning According to dream lore, if you dream of having a wooden leg you will have many new worries. Fortunately, this is a very rare dream.

LETTER (SEE ALSO GIFT)

Psychological Meaning To receive a letter in your dream may herald an unexpected change in your life, such as a new opportunity or challenge. Your response to it indicates the nature of these anticipated events. If it makes you feel good, then you feel assured about the future, but if the contents cause anxiety, it may indicate that you need to take a more positive attitude. The letter could also be from your unconscious mind, which is trying to give you a message about your behavior or your circumstances. Take note of the great wisdom and guidance that come from this hidden source.

Mystical Meaning Some say that dreams of letters foretell unexpected news, but others claim they prophesy a marriage.

LIBRARY

Psychological Meaning A library may represent your desire to learn more and gain new knowledge. It may also represent the knowledge you have accumulated over the years. It is the world of ideas that you explore in your dreams. If people talk in the library or you fail to find the books you want, it may indicate a need for greater concentration or discrimination.

Mystical Meaning According to the wise women of yore, this dream predicts that you will deceive your friends.

LIFT (SEE ALSO ELEVATOR)

Psychological Meaning A lift coming up from a basement may show ideas arising from the unconscious. Going high in a lift may indicate a more elevated and detached viewpoint. You may be more rational, but be careful not to lose touch with your instinct and intuition.

Mystical Meaning The ancient sages took the stairs. However, modern superstition claims that to dream of traveling in a lift means success if it goes up, but disappointment if it goes down.

LIGHT

Psychological Meaning The appearance of light in dreams symbolizes consciousness. Light confirms that profound insights are illuminating or about to illuminate your conscious mind. Light can also take various forms. As a rainbow it symbolizes hope; as sunlight, happiness; and as moonlight, it is the guidance that comes from the unconscious, intuitive part of yourself.

Mystical Meaning The light you see may have a deep, spiritual significance. It may represent your journey toward enlightenment or be a direct experience of the inner light described by mystics. The light may have religious associations with Christ, as the light of the world; the boundless light of the Buddha's Nirvana; or the "light of ten thousand suns," as described in the yoga sutras.

LIGHTHOUSE

Psychological Meaning The lighthouse symbolizes guidance. It helps you safely journey the stormy seas of the unconscious. Consider what it is that has helped you. Perhaps you have met someone in waking life who has guided you, or you have discovered a philosophy or religion to light your way and keep you from the rocks of despair.

Mystical Meaning You will have many new opportunities to choose from, say the oracles.

LEADING

LIGHTNING

Psychological Meaning Lightning can suggest the emotional shock experienced from sudden, unexpected events. Lightning can be destructive, yet it can also show the illuminating brilliance of inspiration. You may be "struck" by a great idea or insight. Lightning also symbolizes the awesome power of nature and suggests that many of the forces governing your life remain beyond your control.

Mystical Meaning Gods of thunder and lightning have appeared in the earliest mythologies. Some authorities believe that these ancient gods were the original gods of Neolithic man preserved in the stories and legends that were passed on from generation to generation. Like many symbols in archaic myths, lightning may be a sexual symbol. When lightning strikes the ground, it represents Mother Earth being impregnated by the sky god.

LION

Psychological Meaning Lions are usually a regal dream symbol of power and pride. In a woman's dream, a lion may represent the male aspect of her psyche. A Freudian interpretation may consider lions the powerful and admired aspect of the father. It may also symbolize your animal nature or aggressiveness and will to power.

Mystical Meaning In the Tarot, the Lion is a symbol of strength that can be controlled by gentleness (symbolized by a woman dressed in white). Astrology says that Leo, the sign of the Lion, is gregarious and likes to be the center of attention. Perhaps your dream is saying that you are displaying these egocentric qualities.

LOAN

Psychological Meaning The dream may simply be about your money worries. This dream can also suggest that you draw too heavily upon your emotional resources. You may feel that you are too self-reliant and now need a little help and support from your friends.

Mystical Meaning A quaint old English superstition claims that if you dream of laughing while returning a loan, you will attract great good luck.

LOST

Psychological Meaning According to some psychologists, dreams about being lost frequently symbolize the beginning of a new phase of life and express the anxiety of leaving behind the familiar. Your dream may also express your worries about having no direction to your life. At times like this, it is wise to make a simple written list of the things that you want to achieve in life. Set yourself an attainable goal; set a deadline; and go for it!

If you dream of losing something, ask yourself what it symbolizes about yourself. For example, if you dream of losing money it may show that you feel you've lost your self-confidence or something you value about yourself.

Mystical Meaning One dusty old dream book warns that to dream of losing something means you may cut yourself by accident.

LOTTERY

Psychological Meaning To dream of winning the lottery may be your way of having an inner holiday. For a few short hours, all your material troubles are over. However, keep a careful note of the numbers—for I've met someone who dreamed of winning and did!

Mystical Meaning Most of the superstitions claim that it is unlucky to dream of the lottery.

L.S.D. (*SEE* PILL)

LUGGAGE

Psychological Meaning Luggage may represent your responsibilities. It may also symbolize the worries, habits, and attitudes you carry around with you. Perhaps you should lighten your load and become a little more carefree. If you dream of giving your luggage to someone else, it may show a need to delegate responsibility.

Mystical Meaning You may have too many material possessions, desires, worries, and needs weighing you down and slowing your spiritual progress. My guru Sathya Sai Baba says, "Less luggage gives more comfort and makes travel a pleasure. Reduce your desires, and this journey to Sai can become a real pleasure for you." Diminishing the luggage (shedding desires) is *Vairagya*. If you lessen your desires, life's journey will be comfortable.

MADNESS

Psychological Meaning Your dream may be telling you that you have been behaving in an inappropriate way. Have you recently experienced a moment of madness? Perhaps you secretly feel that you are too conventional and want to throw away the shackles of routine behavior.

Mystical Meaning Fortune smiles on you if you dream of meeting a lunatic. The oracles say it means you will meet someone of great influence who will help you become prosperous. In Japan, it is believed that if you dream your hair is on fire you will go completely bonkers.

MAN

Psychological Meaning For a man, a male figure may be a symbol for himself. For a woman, he represents the other half of her personality—the side that is rational, intellectual, competitive, aggressive, and analytical, according to Jungian dream interpretation.

Mystical Meaning If he is handsome, everything will be fine, you may even become rich; but if he's as ugly as sin, watch out—problems with friends are ahead.

MANDALA (SEE ALSO NUMBERS)

Psychological Meaning Psychologist Carl Jung noticed that many of his patients' dreams contained geometrical shapes such as triangles, squares, and circles. He realized that these had great significance. As his patients progressed toward psychological health, they dreamed of shapes progressively more symmetrical, with squares and circles radiating in intricate patterns from a central point. Jung understood that similar symbolism could be found in the geometrical patterns and religious diagrams that Tibetan Buddhists, Hindus, and Taoists used as a focus for meditation. These mandalas, as they are called in the East, represent the unity and wholeness of the psyche that is as beautiful and complex as an unfolding flower. Mandalas are your dream signposts to higher consciousness.

Mystical Meaning The mandala represents the oneness of the psyche with the cosmos. Inner and outer become the same. Tibetan Buddhists still use mandalas as a focus of concentration, and some adepts can even sustain the image of a mandala in their mind's eye as they sleep. Certain mandalas are claimed to release magical powers.

MARKET

Psychological Meaning A market may represent your career. It may show what you can offer the world. Similarly, it may illustrate what you have to trade in order to achieve your goals. For example, do you have to trade your domestic happiness for business success? The goods sold in the market may clarify the dream's theme. Antiques may represent your past; fruits and vegetables may show your potential for inner growth; and cheap goods may show that you undervalue your talents.

Mystical Meaning Superstition says that to dream of a market denotes thrift. For a young woman it foretells changes.

MARRIAGE (SEE WEDDING)

MASK

Psychological Meaning A mask represents the way that you present yourself to the world. Do you "put on a brave face" or "mask your feelings"? Psychologists call this psychological mask the *persona*. The danger comes when you forget your true identity and believe you really are the person you have been pretending to be. If you identify with it too closely, mistaking it for the real self, it will appear in your dreams as an artificial being, such as a scarecrow or robot. Ask yourself why you are wearing a mask. What does the face say about the way you present yourself to the world? The nature of the mask may reveal to you that you are pretending an emotion you do not feel or hiding your real feelings. Have the courage to be the person you really are.

Mystical Meaning Muhammad, the founder of Islam, used dreams as a way of explaining the faith. He relates in the Koran a dream in which the angel Gabriel takes him up to heaven riding a silvery-gray mare and where Allah gives him instructions. Arabic works are full of amazing dream insights. This one may help you understand your dream about masks: "He whose soul is pure is never deceived by his dreams, whereas he whose soul is blemished is continually deluded."

MAZE

Psychological Meaning To enter a maze in a dream usually relates to the descent into the unconscious part of yourself. It may show the complex defenses that your conscious mind has put up to prevent your unconscious desires from coming into the light. The path to self-discovery does not follow a straight line, but involves occasional returns to earlier starting points. Your waking life may be particularly complicated at the moment, and you may feel that you're covering the same ground repeatedly.

Mystical Meaning The maze in mythology is a place of transformation where the destructive tendencies of nature are overcome. A classical example of this inner transformation is found in the Greek myth of Theseus and Ariadne overcoming the Minotaur in the labyrinth.

MELTING

Psychological Meaning You may have met someone who is "melting your heart," or maybe you feel that you can stop being intractable and stubborn. If snow is melting, it may show that your icy feelings are becoming a little warmer. You have been emotionally cool for too long, but now you're starting to thaw out. Similarly, you may feel that a restrictive and emotionally paralyzing situation is beginning to ease.

Mystical Meaning According to superstition, melting gold brings sadness, melting silver indicates money problems, and melting ice indicates that a situation is getting out of control.

MERMAID (SEE ALSO ANIMA/ANIMUS, SEA)

Psychological Meaning The mermaid symbolizes the anima—the female aspect of the male psyche. Part woman, part fish, she embodies the mystery that haunts the male psyche. She is the bringer of secret wisdom from the depths of the unconscious, represented by the sea. She is also the seductive siren who may lure the active male energies of the conscious mind into the uncharted depths of the unconscious. A man who dreams of a mermaid may have fears of being drowned by the feminine or by the unconscious. In a woman's dream, a mermaid might express doubts about her femininity. In some dreams, a mermaid can represent a fear of sex.

Mystical Meaning Mythology has many figures that are part human, part animal. The upper half represents the conscious ego, but the lower, fish half is still primitive, irrational, and in need of conscious attention. (A similar comparison can be made with the centaur or Pan.) These mystical symbols were invented to show that the animal and human nature are inseparable.

MESSAGE (SEE LETTER)

MICE (SEE ALSO RAT)

Psychological Meaning Mice can represent your instincts. They may also be a symbol of timidity. They can also represent the small issues that nibble away at your psychological resources.

Mystical Meaning The plague of mice and rats in the *Pied Piper of Hamelin* can be interpreted as an allegory for instincts overcoming rational thought.

MILK

Psychological Meaning This dream may represent your maternal instincts. Similarly, it may represent mother love or nurturing of ideas. If you dream of drinking milk, it may show your need for spiritual sustenance. If you dream of giving milk to others, it may show that you are teaching spiritual values or giving spiritual inspiration to others.

Mystical Meaning To dream of drinking milk is an omen of good health, particularly if it is a mother's milk.

MIRROR

Psychological Meaning What you dream of seeing in the mirror is the way you see yourself or the way that you want others to see you. You may not like what you see. Many people have the alarming dream of looking in the mirror and seeing someone else's face reflected there. This sudden fear of not knowing who you are produces an identity crisis. What face did you see? The person, animal, or object you saw will give ried by this dream. It demonstrates that you are progressing in the journey of self-discovery. You are prepared to look at yourself. Next, you may want to make changes to your behavior. However, if the person in the mirror has his or her eyes closed, then this indicates that you are unwilling to face reality.

Mystical Meaning An ancient and widespread superstition held that the reflection of a person seen in a glass was actually their soul. For this reason, Dracula has no reflection.

MIXING

Psychological Meaning To dream of mixing chemicals, potions, or even a cocktail is a metaphor to show, not the entrance of a new element to life, but a mixing of elements already there. For example, it can show the blending of opposite sides of your personality and may imply that you should adopt an attitude that is more flexible. One school of thought interprets this blending as the interaction of the left and right sides of the brain, representing logic and intuition.

Mystical Meaning The Tarot card Temperance shows an angel pouring water from one chalice to another and the Star card shows a woman pouring water into a pool and onto the land beside her. Similarly, the zodiacal sign Aquarius is represented by a water-bearer. Like your dream, these images symbolize the flow of life; the essential connection between conscious and unconscious; and the blending of male and female elements.

MONEY (SEE ALSO TREASURE)

Psychological Meaning Dreaming of a lack of money can symbolize a lack of the abilities or qualifications needed to achieve some desired goal. Hoarding money can indicate selfishness, whereas to dream of sharing money can symbolize magnanimity.

Mystical Meaning It was considered fortunate to dream of receiving or finding money, suggesting that good fortune is coming your way. Some superstitions say that to dream of finding money means a birth.

MONK

Psychological Meaning A monk may represent devotion, piety, and religious feelings. He could symbolize your need for a period of solitude. In a man's dream, he may represent the spiritual self.

Mystical Meaning Superstitions claim that to dream of a monk foretells unpleasant journeys and dissension in the family.

MONKEY

Psychological Meaning Monkeys represent your playful, mischievous side. You may feel that your dream expresses a need to be fun-loving and to stop taking life so seriously. Monkeys can also represent an immature attitude or repressed sexuality.

Mystical Meaning My Indian guru, Sathya Sai Baba, teases his followers by calling them "monkey mind" every time they give in to untamed worries, doubts, and fears. However, the constantly chattering monkey mind can be stilled by meditation. Your dream may be showing you the way to find this perfect inner peace.

MONSTER (SEE ALSO GIANT)

Psychological Meaning Towering, monstrous figures often occur in children's dreams. These figures usually represent adults in the child's life who dominate him or her with what must seem like invincible power. Children (and adults) are advised to confront these dream monsters in order to come to terms with their emotional lives.

Mystical Meaning The old dream books say that to dream of slaying a monster denotes that you will overcome enemies and rise to prominence. In ancient Tibet, wrathful monsters were considered to be guardian deities. They symbolized the powers within the self that could deter and destroy ignorance.

MOON

Psychological Meaning From time immemorial the moon has been regarded as the source of fertility, as it governs tides, rainfall, birth, and menstruation. Within dreams, it can therefore symbolize the possibility of personal growth.

The moon usually represents the feminine aspect of the self and anything hidden or mysterious. Its association with water also identifies it with the imagination. A full moon may indicate completion whereas a new moon symbolizes new beginnings. An eclipse of the moon may show that your feminine side is being overshadowed by something. A Freudian interpretation of this would say that an eclipse represents getting rid of the attachment to your mother that is detrimental to your personal growth. If the moon eclipses the sun, it may show that unconscious forces are overpowering the conscious ego.

Mystical Meaning   Palmistry tells that the lunar region of the hand (opposite the thumb) is the area where you find the lines of travel. To dream of the moon may therefore indicate a journey ahead. It is likely to be across water.

MOTHER

Psychological Meaning   The mother may symbolize the unconscious, intuitive side of yourself. However, the mother symbol can take both positive or negative forms. She may appear as a kindly mother, grandmother, or aunt or as a place, such as a cave, church, or garden. These images may represent the qualities of solicitude, growth, nourishment, and fertility. The negative mother symbol may appear as a witch or a dragon and represents dark, destructive tendencies that devour, seduce, or poison. Some people have problems freeing themselves from mother-attachment. This prevents the development of their individuality and inner self-dependence.

Mystical Meaning   Most mystical traditions have the symbol of the mother written into their legends and myths. At her most exalted, she is the divine Great Mother. At her most frightening, she is the gorgon Medusa or the Sumerian goddess Lilith. Freud believed that the Greek myths of Oedipus and Electra symbolized psychological conditions. Oedipus killed his father and married his mother. Freud claimed that this represented a boy's incestuous desire for his

mother and his jealousy toward his father. Similarly, Electra desired her father and was jealous of her mother. A girl may therefore unconsciously believe that she has been castrated by her mother and is now an incomplete male. According to Freud, this gives rise to penis-envy, said to be one of the root causes of women's feelings of inferiority.

MOUNTAIN

Psychological Meaning   Mountains represent the lofty planes of consciousness, the realm of the higher self, the part of you that has transcendent knowledge. Dreaming of being at the top of a mountain may show that you feel now that you have risen above the common routines of life and achieved something with spiritual meaning. Conversely, it may show your desire to do this. Mountains can also indicate that you are in touch with or thinking about the higher dimensions of reality. In particular you may be thinking in a positive way about death and the afterlife. On a more mundane level, climbing a mountain may symbolize your sense of achievement and the arduous effort needed for a long-term undertaking. You are on the slippery slopes to success and have the self-determination to reach the summit.

Mystical Meaning   If you dream of climbing a mountain effortlessly, then all your ventures will be successful, but if you fail in your efforts to reach the summit your plans will fail. To the Chinese, a mountain can symbolize the unshakable peace that comes from keeping the mind still during meditation.

MOUTH

Psychological Meaning   Words can heal and harm. Your dream may be saying something about harsh words that have been spoken. Or you may be reminded of something said to you recently. Perhaps you said something you shouldn't have. A mouth may also symbolize your need to express yourself or talk about an issue that's troubling you. Perhaps a part of your personality needs to express itself? Freud, of course, believed the mouth to be a sexual symbol

MONEY

representing the vagina. He also said that to dream about mouths may represent a childhood fixation marked by immature characteristics such as verbal aggression.

Mystical Meaning It is claimed that a large mouth shows riches to come but a small mouth betokens poverty. To see someone with a twisted or misshapen mouth foretells a family quarrel.

MURDER

Psychological Meaning If you dream of murdering someone you know, this dream may reveal your hidden feelings of resentment toward that person. Similarly, the person being murdered could represent an aspect of yourself you are trying to repress or destroy. What is it about yourself that you are trying to kill off? If you are the one being murdered, it may show that you are at the mercy of your emotions. Perhaps you have repressed your instincts that are now seeking vengeance.

Mystical Meaning The jury's still out on this one. Some oracles claim that this dream foretells sorrow, but others say it has no prophetic significance.

MUSEUM

Psychological Meaning A museum may represent the history of yourself and your past. It exhibits all of the important events that have made you into the person you are today. It can also represent the archaic world of the collective unconscious.

Mystical Meaning To dream of being in a museum denotes a period ahead of unhappiness and boredom, say some dream soothsayers.

MUSIC

Psychological Meaning Music is the opposite of chaos. In dreams, it represents harmony and the infinite potential of creative life. Your dream music can also express the emotions you are feeling at the moment. Is the tone happy, tragic, sad,

or threatening? Also, take note of any words and consider whether the tunes you hear have any personal associations. If the music you hear is discordant, it may suggest that your creative potential has become distorted. Many of the great composers claimed that they spontaneously heard their greatest works while dreaming or immediately after waking.

Mystical Meaning The pipes of Pan, the Pied Piper, and the haunting call of the Harpies all express the closeness of the unconscious inner realm to the world of death. Mystics also talk of the music of the spheres, the ethereal music that symbolizes the harmony of the cosmos. It is said that sometimes people hear the songs of the angels in dreams.

NAIL

Psychological Meaning A nail may represent the fact that you have resolved an issue; you have "hit the nail on the head." It could also be a phallic symbol. If nails are driven into your hands, it may show that you feel you are a martyr to your emotions or ideals. Calm, even-tempered thinking is recommended.

Mystical Meaning Since Roman times, iron has been believed to be a sacred metal. To dream of a rusty iron nail is therefore very lucky.

NAKED (SEE ALSO NUDITY)

Psychological Meaning To dream of being naked may indicate that you feel vulnerable and exposed. You may feel that you are unable to maintain your defenses against the outside world.

Mystical Meaning This dream can mean innocence or, if you are a traditional Christian, can refer to the Last Judgement.

NAMES

Psychological Meaning Names can sometimes contain puns that reveal the meaning of your dream. For example, a Mr. Swift may be your dream telling you to hurry up and put your plans into action. Dreams set in Washington may suggest you should be careful what you say. (Washing tongue!) The puns may be bad, but they reveal the hidden meaning of your dream.

Mystical Meaning There are specific superstitions associated with names. For example, if you dream that your name is George you will never be hanged. But if it's Agnes, you will go mad!

NEEDLE

Psychological Meaning Being pricked by a needle may represent the minor irritations and worries that upset you. Perhaps something is needling you? Sewing with a needle may represent your desire to repair the damage caused by a past hurt. And of course, Freud would observe that a needle is a phallic symbol.

Mystical Meaning Generally, this dream is believed to foretell a disappointment. In some parts of the world, it is said to be unlucky to mention the word needle when you wake up in the morning.

NEST

Psychological Meaning A nest may represent your home and your domestic life. It is also the place where eggs are incubated, so there's a promise that you are hatching new ideas or making new opportunities.

Mystical Meaning Dreaming of a nest full of eggs denotes that you will be prosperous. An Austrian superstition claims that to dream of a nest foretells that you will get a boil.

NIGHT

Psychological Meaning The night can represent the unconscious side of the personality. It can also symbolize ignorance, evil, or the despair of the "dark night of the soul." The process of becoming sometimes involves entering the darkness before emerging into light.

Mystical Meaning An old superstition says that you can avoid nightmares by hanging your socks or stockings over the end of the bed with a pin stuck through them. The Gypsies say that to dream of the night shows despair unless you see a wagon, campfire, or a star-studded sky.

NOISE

Psychological Meaning Noise may be your own thoughts that talk in an endless inner dialogue. Meditation techniques practiced before retiring can help to increase inner peace and still your chattering mind. Noise may also be your unconscious trying to attract your attention and make you examine an issue.

Mystical Meaning Some oracles claim that to dream of a loud noises predicts you will soon get a new job.

Common Dream

NUDITY (SEE ALSO UNDRESSED IN PUBLIC)

I dream that I am directing the traffic. To my horror, I suddenly realize that I am naked but to my surprise, nobody notices me.—B.G., Edinburgh, Scotland

NUDITY

Psychological Meaning Many sleepers are embarrassed to find themselves dreaming of being in a public place and being either naked or wearing only their underwear. These dreams often express feelings of guilt or inferiority. It is a metaphor that exposes the dreamer's perceived faults or feelings of vulnerability to some situation in life. In the above example, the fact that other people are oblivious to the dreamer's nudity indicates that the dreamer should discard as groundless any fears of being rejected if the real self is revealed. To dream of being ashamed or frightened of being naked may indicate a fear of relationships or of showing your real feelings. (Sigmund Freud once said that his favorite dream was being naked in a crowd of strangers!)

A dream of being disgusted by the nudity of another person suggests anxiety or aversion at discovering the naked truth about a person, a situation, or even about yourself. Acceptance of the nudity of others indicates that you see through people and accept them for what they are.

Nudity can also represent your longing for the lost innocence of childhood. It represents the real you stripped of pretense and imposed social conditioning. Nudity also has spiritual connotations; it is an expression of beauty and divinity. The ancient gods, such as Venus the goddess of love, Diana the goddess of the hunt, or the three Muses, who inspire the artist, are all usually depicted naked.

ASK YOURSELF

1. *Do I want people to see me for the person I really am?* It's usually the best policy to be yourself despite what you fear others may think. Examine the attitude of other people in the dream. Their behavior may reveal what attitudes are holding you back from being the person you really are.

2. *Do I feel guilty about something?* Often these dreams reveal a fear of being exposed. For example, have you been cheating in some way? Perhaps you have been putting up pretence or lying about something you fear someone may find out about.

3. *Do I fear disapproval?* You may fear that a plan will meet with disapproval from your colleagues. This may be particularly relevant if you dream of being naked at work.

Mystical Meaning Mothers used to warn their daughters that to dream of being naked meant that the dreamer would soon hear about a terrible scandal. However, the Gypsies believed that good fortune awaited the person who dreamed of being naked, particularly if it the dream was lit by the stars.

NUMBERS (*SEE ALSO* MANDALA)

Psychological Meaning Numbers and their corresponding geometric shapes often occur in dreams. They can represent stages of spiritual growth and archetypal energies of the collective unconscious.

Zero: Zero represents the unmanifested void. It is the ineffable vastness of space, infinite and timeless. Its symbol is the circle, the perfect mandala.

One: One is the number that initiates action. It may represent the source of life or oneness of all creation. Its associated shape is a point.

Two: Two represents diversity. It is the number of duality and divine symmetry. It represents the union of opposites such as male and female, mother and father, yin and yang, or heaven and earth.

Three: Considered by the ancient Greeks to be the perfect number, three represents the union of body, mind, and spirit. Its shape is the triangle, which may represent the creative force. Three can also symbolize the Holy Trinity.

$$5 \, 8^3 \mathbf{2} \, 7^9$$

Four: Symbolized by the square, four is the number of stability and harmony. It may also relate to the four seasons, the four elements, and Jung's four mental functions of thought, feeling, sense, and intuition.

Five: Five represents the link between the heavens and the earth. Its symbol is the five-pointed pentagram.

Six: Six symbolizes inner harmony and perfection. It may be represented by a hexagram or the six-pointed Star of David.

Seven: Seven is the symbol of completeness—an idea originating from the belief that the world was created in six days and finished by the seventh. It was believed that the soul renewed itself every seven years, and hence the belief that to break a mirror will bring seven years' bad luck, as mirrors are a reflection of the soul.

Eight: The Chinese believe that eight is very lucky and brings great good fortune. It can represent regeneration and new beginnings.

Nine: In India, this is the number of God and the yogi, who will leave the wheel of birth and death. In the West, it is also considered to be the number of eternity.

Ten: As there are Ten Commandments, the number ten was considered the number of the law.

Mystical Meaning Numerology is the study of the mystical meaning of numbers. Originally based on the Hebrew and Greek alphabets, it attributed a number to each letter, so that words and names could be studied for their mystical meaning. Holy books such as the Bible are full of numerological references. When the numerical equivalents of a person's name or birth date are added together, the numbers obtained can tell a great deal about the person's character, qualities, skills, and destiny. The art of numerology has sometimes been applied to dreams to obtain information about the future.

The human qualities associated with each name number are: *one*, initiation; *two*, attractiveness; *three*, communicator; *four*, homemaker; *five*, experience; *six*, calmness; *seven*, philosopher; *eight*, business; *nine*, freedom.

NUN
Psychological Meaning A nun may represent purity and chastity. To dream of a nun may symbolize a need to find spiritual meaning.
Mystical Meaning If you dream of being a nun you will experience disappointment in love, but if you meet a nun the reverse is true.

NUT
Psychological Meaning A nut may represent the ego that must be destroyed before the spiritual self can emerge. A green nut cannot be opened, but when a nut is ready one little tap will do. In the same way, enlightenment comes when the time is ripe.
Mystical Meaning According to superstition, to dream of nuts is a sign that money is coming.

 OBSTACLE
Psychological Meaning Dreaming of obstacles to your progress can indicate that you are uncertain of your ability to achieve your goals in life. You lack self-confidence and may feel unable to do the things you want to do. You may feel that you are being tested in some way. The barrier may or may not be self-imposed. It may represent a social distinction or some inner difficulty that is restricting your self-expression.
Mystical Meaning Ramana Maharshi said: "There are no impediments to meditation. The very thought of such obstacles is the greatest impediment." And so too with your dream: imagined obstacles always seem so much bigger than real ones.

OCEAN (SEE SEA)

OEDIPUS (SEE MOTHER)

OFFICE
Psychological Meaning A dream set in a working environment is most likely to be describing your conduct and the way you present yourself to the world. Offices are also organized places with everything neatly filled (we hope). The dream may be telling you to be more organized.
Mystical Meaning If you dream of being happy in an office, it is a sign of prosperity. If you are turned out of an office, expect disappointments.

OIL
Psychological Meaning You may feel that your life has ground to a halt, and oil symbolizes what it is you need to get your inner machinery moving again. The dream may be suggesting that you need to socialize or do something to break the emotional deadlock.

Mystical Meaning Superstition says that if a man dreams he is dealing in oil, he will be rich—but unsuccessful at lovemaking.

OINTMENT

Psychological Meaning This is probably a symbol of healing. Something may have entered your life that feels like a soothing balm and that relieves your bruises from the past.
Mystical Meaning Dreaming of ointment predicts that you will make new friends.

OPENING

Psychological Meaning Opening something can symbolize a new influence entering your life. You may feel inspired with new ideas soon. Ask yourself whether you are opening yourself to beneficial spiritual influences or less savory ones.
Mystical Meaning To dream of opening a door denotes slander from enemies.

OPPONENT

Psychological Meaning An opponent may be an aspect of yourself. You may have an inner conflict or be wrestling with a problem.
Mystical Meaning It is said to be unlucky to dream of triumphing over an opponent, for it shows you have malicious enemies who will succeed in harming you.

OPPOSITES

Psychological Meaning Opposites in a dream represent the opposite qualities of the psyche. This can include masculine and feminine, extrovert and introvert, active and passive, and will be represented by symbols such as light and dark, left and right, man and woman, etc. The brain is split into two distinctive hemispheres that have different functions. Dreams may help to bring these functions together as one harmonious whole.

Mystical Meaning The yogi resolves the opposites by merging with the infinite (Brahman). Reflect on the meaning of your dream in the light of this quote from the *Bhagavad Gita*: "By passion for the 'pairs of opposites.' By those twin snares of Like and Dislike, Prince, All creatures live bewildered, save some few who, quit of sins, holy in act, informed, Freed from the 'opposites' and fixed in faith, cleave unto me."

ORANGE (*SEE* COLORS)

ORPHAN

Psychological Meaning Your dream may be saying that you feel lonely, unloved, and rejected. Alternatively, the orphan may represent some part of yourself that you have rejected.
Mystical Meaning Dreams of orphans foretell profits from rich acquaintances but unhappiness in matters of the heart.

OVEN

Psychological Meaning Something's cooking. The oven may offer a promise of nourishment in the future. For the time being you have to wait for your reward. A Freudian interpretation is that an oven represents the womb and can be a symbol for pregnancy. You may be giving birth to new ideas and may be expressing a new attitude.
Mystical Meaning To dream you are cooking at an oven is a sign of a change. If the oven is hot, the change will be for the good, but if it's cold, watch out!

OWL

Psychological Meaning An owl may symbolize the wisdom that is gained from the nocturnal world of the unconscious.
Mystical Meaning Superstition says that this is a melancholy dream predicting sadness, poverty, and sometimes disgrace.

PAIN

Psychological Meaning Your dream may be triggered by a physical ache. Dreams can reveal a great deal about health and give warnings about potential illness. As well as diagnosing, they sometimes give remedies, such as a change in diet or lifestyle. As a symbol, pain occurring in a dream may represent the emotional hurt you feel at the moment.

Mystical Meaning Some dream oracles claim that to feel pain in a dream means that a trivial transaction will cause a great deal of unhappiness. Other oracles contradict this and say that it means unexpected money is coming your way. Perhaps the key to success is to be careful.

PAINTING (*SEE ALSO* COLORS)

Psychological Meaning To dream of painting may symbolize your need to express your creative potential. However, it may also show the way you picture your situation. What is shown on your canvas or paper? Are the colors bright or drab? Is there a dominance of one hue? For example, reds may indicate that you are feeling aggressive, whereas blues may show a period of melancholy.

Mystical Meaning If you dream of painting, it means you will be pleased with your present occupation, but if you get any paint on your clothes you will be criticized by others.

PAPER

Psychological Meaning To dream of a clean white sheet of paper may symbolize your desire to make a new start in life. It could also represent your desire to express yourself through writing or art. If the paper is a document of some kind, it may refer to something in your past. A common anxiety dream for people in authority is to dream of a desk stacked high with papers. This suggests that you are finding it almost impossible to cope with the stress and demands that come with responsibility. Are you dealing effectively with incoming work? You may want to consider delegating some of your work load.

Mystical Meaning According to the dream oracles, to dream of blank paper foretells a period of grief. However, paper with writing on it predicts great joy concerning a love affair.

PARADISE

Psychological Meaning Paradise may represent the state of spiritual perfection that you wish to achieve. It may also be your dream's way of giving you a temporary respite from the troubles of the real world.

Mystical Meaning If your dream of paradise includes palm trees, the good fortune of this auspicious dream is doubled. Sailors believe that this is a dream of safe travel and good luck.

PARALYSIS

Psychological Meaning You may feel that you are unable to act to deal with a situation or inner problem. It is likely that your own attitudes and emotional baggage are making you unable to act. You may have fears or anxieties about a general or specific issue that are troubling you in more ways than you admit. For every problem, there is a solution. Keep a careful note of your dreams for the rest of the week; they may offer solutions to help you resolve your hidden anxieties. If you dream of someone else being paralyzed, they may represent an aspect of yourself that is not being given free expression. Similarly, if you dream of a paralyzed animal, your instincts and sexual feelings may be inhibited. (Some psychologists claim that repeatedly dreaming of paralysis is a sign that your diet needs changing.)

Mystical Meaning It was once believed that the "nightmare" was a huge spirit that sat on people while they slept. The feeling of being paralyzed was caused because of this demon. In Europe, the solution was to sleep with a knife near the bed because evil spirits feared iron and steel.

PARCEL

Psychological Meaning What you take out of the parcel may represent the parts of yourself that you are becoming aware of. This may be a time of self-discovery. It may also be a symbol for your hidden talents. You may be a very "gifted" person and should use your latent abilities.

Mystical Meaning You will have a surprise meeting with someone you've not seen for a long time if you dream of receiving a parcel.

PARTY

Psychological Meaning This dream can indicate the pleasures of life and particularly social interaction. You may simply feel that you need to get out more and enjoy the company of others. The nature of the party and your feelings will reveal your hidden hopes and fears. For example, a happy party may indicate that you feel self-confident, but a bad one may indicate that you are unsure of your social skills. A formal party may represent your working life, whereas an orgy may be expressing your sexual frustrations.

Mystical Meaning Traditional interpretations say that this dream indicates that quarrels are ahead unless the party is exceptionally enjoyable.

PASSENGER

Psychological Meaning You may feel that some of your friends and family take a parasitical attitude toward you. Are you spending too much of your available energy carrying others? If you are a passenger, it may indicate that you are not in control of your life. Are you always meekly going along with other people's decisions?

Mystical Meaning If you see passengers laden with luggage coming toward you, you will see an improvement in your situation. If they are traveling away from you, conditions will deteriorate.

PASSPORT

Psychological Meaning A passport represents your identity. It may symbolize a period of self-analysis and the need to know your true nature. A passport takes you to foreign lands and the undiscovered world of the unconscious. You may be about to embark on an inner journey of self-discovery.

Mystical Meaning According to some oracles, dreaming of passports has nothing to do with travel. It means your love life will blossom!

PATH

Psychological Meaning This dream may represent your progress and the paths you are taking through life. The references may be to both psychological and material conditions. This may be a good time to reassess your future goals and consider what you most want from life.

Mystical Meaning A broad, smooth pathway indicates emotional troubles, but a rocky road predicts a happy marriage.

PATIENT

Psychological Meaning The dream may be suggesting that you are undergoing a healing process. Alternatively, it could be a pun to say you must have more patience.

Mystical Meaning To dream of being a patient indicates that a happy surprise is coming your way.

PAYING

Psychological Meaning This dream may show that you are taking charge of your situation. You are paying your own way.

Mystical Meaning Paying may show the workings of karma—cause and effect. Everything has its cost: gluttony brings ill health; selfishness brings loneliness; material greed brings spiritual poverty; and so on. The key to happiness is to find the middle way between craving and austerity. Accept that you can possess nothing. It all belongs to God, who loans you the things of this world. Dedicate the fruits of your labor to God and you will possess nothing and yet have everything.

FAMOUS DREAMER

Napoleon Bonaparte
Emperor of France

Napoleon probably said "Not tonight, Josephine," because he was so busy scribbling down his dreams! He was said to have used them to plan his military campaigns. Before the battle of Waterloo, he supposedly had a dream about a black cat that ran between opposing armies. As it did this, he saw his own forces decimated.

On June 18, 1815, Napoleon was finally defeated at Waterloo by British, Dutch, Belgian, and German forces commanded by the Duke of Wellington.

PEN/PENCIL

Psychological Meaning Pens and pencils are probably used in your dream as phallic symbols. However, they are also symbols of self-expression. Take careful note of anything you write or see written in the dream. This may be a cryptic message from your unconscious.

Mystical Meaning Dream lore says that if you dream of a pen that will not write, you'll be charged with a serious breach of morality!

PEOPLE

Psychological Meaning If you dream of people you know, your unconscious may be making you aware of qualities and feelings that you desire. The feelings that your interaction with those people gives will be those you are becoming aware of in real life. If you dream of people you don't know, it may be a way of confronting aspects of yourself. Ask yourself what the dream says about the hidden aspects of yourself. Do you like the person in the dream? What does this person mean to you?

Mystical Meaning So long as the people you meet are friendly and well dressed, you can expect good fortune, say the dream books of old.

PHALLUS

Psychological Meaning Dreams often express sexual feelings that society would never permit in reality. Sometimes these instincts are repressed or pushed out of conscious awareness. In dreams, your primal instincts and desires (the id) try to communicate with the conscious ego. Freud says that this communication is censored by the super-ego, your moral principle. The result is that the sexual messages from the unconscious come through to the conscious mind in the disguised form of symbols. Phallic symbols can include anything long and straight that may resemble the male penis.

Mystical Meaning In many races and tribes, the phallus is the primary symbol of worship. Ancient cave paintings of the human reproductive organs have been found in countries as far apart as Senegal and Niger, Australia, France, China, Japan, and India. They are proof of the power of this symbol. For example, the Romans used phallic charms to ward off evil spirits and the god Priapus was depicted as a huge phallus with a human face. The Toltecs and Aztecs of Mexico worshiped a winged snake, and the Hindus still worship Shiva as a phallic emblem. The favorite god in Chinese homes is Shou-lao, the god of longevity. He is normally depicted with an enormous bald head that resembles a phallus.

PICTURE

Psychological Meaning A portrait or still photograph often suggests that you feel a need to preserve a relationship. You may idealize the past and want it to remain the same forever. A picture may also represent your thoughts or ideas and be a way of making you aware of something that requires your attention. The content of the picture will symbolize what this is.

Mystical Meaning Your hopes are false if you dream of a picture, says superstition. It can also mean disappointment in love, particularly if the picture is of you.

PIG

Psychological Meaning A pig may symbolize ignorance, stubbornness, greed, or just plain bad manners. It can even be a sexual symbol of bestiality and brutish lust. Perhaps you or someone close to you has been behaving like a chauvinistic pig? Of course, this dream has nothing to do with kind police officers or sensitive journalists.

Mystical Meaning Pigs have long been the subject of superstition. For example, fishermen believe that if you say the word "pig" before fishing you will have a poor catch. However, in dreams pigs denote exceptionally good news or a stroke of luck.

PILL

Psychological Meaning You may have realized something that is just the medicine you need to restore inner harmony. If you dream of taking a hallucinogenic drug, this dream may be the start of a series of lucid dreams. An addictive pill may indicate that it is your compulsive emotional behavior that harms you. Alternatively, the pill may represent the bitter pill you have to swallow.

Mystical Meaning Some people believe that hallucinogenic drugs such as LSD can awaken the higher consciousness that is found in deep meditation and sometimes also in dreams. The problem is that what goes up also has to come down. "A man who has attained certain powers through medicines, or through words, or through mortification still has desires, but that man who has attained to *Samadhi* through concentration is alone free from all desires."—Vivekananda.

PIN (SEE NEEDLE)

PLAY

Psychological Meaning Playing emphasizes that your creativity is unrestricted by an overtly serious attitude. You may have an attitude that likes to break the rules of convention. A playful attitude toward work can sometimes be more productive than the drudgery of monotonous repetition.

Mystical Meaning My Indian guru, Sathya Sai Baba, tells us that life is a divine play that the Hindus call *leela*. One of his most well-known sayings is "Life is a dream; realize it. Life is a game; play it."

POISON

Psychological Meaning If you dream of consuming something poisonous, it may indicate that you are introducing something into yourself that is harmful to your well-being. This may be bad feelings or bitterness on your part. Similarly, the poison could represent underhanded actions of others or a fear of being the target of innuendo.

Mystical Meaning As you would expect, superstition says that dreaming of poison indicates that you will suffer because of the wrongdoing of others.

POLICE

Psychological Meaning Laws, rules, and regulations represent structure and control. Dreams in which you break rules may show your urge toward self-assertion and your desire to test the limits imposed by others.

If you dream of being accused of breaking rules of whose existence you were unaware, this shows the unfairness of many life experiences. You may be frustrated by your circumstances and feel that life is unjust. Police officers can symbolize the upholding of rules of conduct. They may represent inhibition and the censorship of natural impulses by the conscious mind. (Freud claimed that police officers were a superego symbol, representing taboos stemming from childhood.)

If you dream of being arrested it may symbolize sexuality or emotions being restrained by feelings of guilt. Alternatively, your dream may be telling you to arrest your feelings and stop behaving in inappropriate or anti-social ways. If you dream of being chased by the police, you may need to face the accusations of a guilty conscience or learn from past mistakes.

Mystical Meaning Tradition says that to dream of a police officer means that you will be helped by someone you love.

PRIEST

Psychological Meaning A priest may represent traditional religion with its spiritual rules and regulations. Are you making moral judgments? Alternatively, the priest could represent your own spiritual wisdom.

Mystical Meaning Any dream concerning a priest is deemed good by superstitious people. In particular it means the end of a quarrel.

PRISON

Psychological Meaning You may feel that your life is restricted at the moment, and your dream reflects your need to change your routines. To release yourself you may need to make major changes to your waking life. Another interpretation is that you are restricted by behavior that enslaves you or you have repressed your emotions. If you dream of someone else in prison, it may represent the element of your personality that you are unable to set free.

Mystical Meaning Superstition can sometimes interpret dreams in very strange ways. One says that if you dream of seeing prisoners it is an omen that soon your dearest wish will be granted. Some sources claim that it predicts a marriage. I wonder why!

PRIZE

Psychological Meaning You may feel pleased with yourself and may be encouraged by your unconscious. You may have made significant progress in your personal development or may have achieved an important worldly goal. Your unconscious is saying, "You can do it. You can win!"

Mystical Meaning Dream of giving or receiving a prize and you'll soon be in the money.

PUNISHMENT

Psychological Meaning You may have a conscience about something that has happened or feel guilty about something. Are you be punishing yourself? Sometimes traumatic childhood experiences or overly authoritarian parents can set in motion a self-punishment cycle that can become an automatic psychological response. You may need to free yourself of the parental and social conditioning that holds you back from being your true self.

If you dream of punishing people you know, you may have a hidden resentment toward them. Alternatively, they may represent aspects of your own personality that you fear. If you dream of punishing an animal, you may feel antagonistic toward your instinctive drives and sexuality. In all instances, you must learn acceptance and forgiveness if you want to be at peace with yourself.

Mystical Meaning The Gypsies believe that to dream of being punished betrays the guilt you feel for neglecting your relations.

PUPPET

Psychological Meaning Either you are trying to control someone or someone is trying to control you. Puppets are manipulated by strings or a hidden hand. Is it you who have the power, or is someone else pulling the strings?

Mystical Meaning The oracles announce that happiness is assured because of your ability to organize people if you dream of puppets.

PURPLE (SEE COLORS)

PURSE

Psychological Meaning The purse is a common symbol for female sexuality. It can stand for both the female genitalia and the womb. According to Freud, as the purse can be both opened and closed, it sometimes represents the female power to give or withhold favors. As the purse is also a place you keep money, it may also symbolize treasure, which can be a symbol for the real self. If you dream of losing your purse, then this may be an allegory for losing touch with your real identity. To dream of an empty purse may indicate a loss of security.

Mystical Meaning If you dream you open your purse and find money in it, you will be happy, particularly if you find gold. Similarly, it is good if you find a purse. But beware if you dream that someone tells you they have found a purse, for this means you will hear bad news soon.

QUARREL

Psychological Meaning You may have an inner conflict or be trying to make a difficult emotional decision. You are divided within yourself. Just as with arguments in real life, a compromise is usually the best course. Stop seeing everything in black-and-white. Alternatively, you may be expressing emotions that you have been unable to give vent to in waking life. If you know the person you are arguing with, he or she may represent an aspect of yourself. Do you secretly resent this person in waking life?

Mystical Meaning Superstition says that this dream portends unhappiness in relationships and business.

QUARRY

Psychological Meaning A quarry is a man-made hole in the environment. Perhaps your dream indicates that you have dug yourself into an emotional hole from which you cannot escape. Have you fallen into a pit of despair? A quarry may also symbolize your desire to reveal the contents of the unconscious, symbolized by the earth. Perhaps you have uncovered something that was once hidden? In a social sense, a quarry may represent your concerns about the damage being done to the environment. (If your quarry was the pursuit of an animal, see Chase.)

Mystical Meaning A chalk quarry is an omen for financial difficulties that can be overcome by hard labor. A stone quarry predicts a journey.

QUEEN (SEE ALSO ANIMA/ANIMUS, KING, MOTHER)

Psychological Meaning Freud believed that the king and queen represent the dreamer's parents, while a prince or princess represent the dreamer. She may stand for the unconscious, intuition, nature, and the instincts. Jung saw royal figures as representations of animus (the male principle) and anima (female principle). The white queen from Lewis Carroll's *Through the Looking-Glass* (1872) runs continuously to stay at the same spot. Some authorities claim she expresses the way the earth is in a continuous state of upheaval in order to stay much the same.

Mystical Meaning Carl Jung recognized that the strange writings of the alchemists were in fact symbols for the integration of the personality. The queen personified the feminine forces within the psyche, the unconscious feeling for life.

RABBIT

Psychological Meaning Because of their reputation for breeding, rabbits may represent your sexual activity. The rabbit could also represent innocence and timidity. If you dream of it going down a hole, this could show that you are trying to escape from a problem.

Mystical Meaning It is a good omen if you dream of seeing rabbits running in green grass. If you see them in hutches, the good fortune will be lessened. Dead bunnies bode disaster.

RACE

Psychological Meaning This dream may be an allegory for the way you live. Are you in a perpetual hurry? The dream may reveal your competitive side and that you measure yourself against other people. Make a conscious decision to slow down and you may achieve more. The old story holds true—the steady progress of the tortoise beats the impulsive hare.

Mystical Meaning If you dream you are racing a car or running, this is a sign that you will soon hear news. If you win, the news will be wonderful.

RADIO

Psychological Meaning What is said or played on the radio may be messages from your unconscious. You are tuning in to its frequency. In particular, note the words of any songs played and consider what these say about the way you are feeling.

Mystical Meaning Not many ancient mystics had radios, but superstitions that are more recent say that listening to one in a dream foretells an imminent meeting.

RAGS

Psychological Meaning If you dream of wearing rags, you may be concerned about your self-image. You may feel unable to deal with responsibilities and may lack self-confidence. You may feel that your life is in tatters. Perhaps a little retail therapy will brighten you up? Buy something new and give yourself a boost.

Mystical Meaning Some oracles predict that you will suffer great losses if you dream of wearing rags. Other authorities claim that it is a sign that you will make a wise decision.

RAILROAD (SEE TRAIN)

RAIN

Psychological Meaning Rain usually represents cleansing and purification. It can also represent the release of tension that comes after a storm or a period of crying. Rain replenishes and brings fertility, so it may also symbolize that you are opening to a new phase of personal growth in your life. Your dream says, "Don't worry, for soon the gray clouds will be gone and light will shine in your life once more."

Mystical Meaning To dream of rain is generally considered a good omen unless of course the rain is falling on cattle, for this means a business loss of some kind.

RAINBOW

Psychological Meaning A rainbow symbolizes good news, hope, redemption and the end of gloom. Since the sun can be a symbol of the self, it is also associated with the magical quest for the treasure of self-knowledge. The rainbow is a bridge between heaven and earth, between your earthly self and your higher, enlightened self.

Mystical Meaning The Gypsies say that to dream of a brightly colored rainbow means a happy change is coming. If the colors become dull there will be a deterioration in your circumstances.

RAPE

Psychological Meaning For a man, this may be a sadistic expression of sexual desire. It may show feelings of vengeance toward the opposite sex. For a woman this dream may represent fears of sex or masochistic fantasies.

Mystical Meaning Even the Victorian dream books cover this topic. Superstition claims that if a woman dreams of rape, her pride will be wounded. You will hear shocking news if you dream that a friend is raped.

RAT (SEE ALSO MICE)

Psychological Meaning Rats may represent unworthy thoughts and feelings that hide from the light of day and gnaw away inside you. These may be feelings of guilt, envy, avarice, and so on, or they may be of a sexual nature. They could represent the feelings you reject. In addition, you may have thoughts about wanting to harm others or perhaps you feel that somebody in your life is, in the words of James Cagney, a "dirty rat."

Mystical Meaning An enemy will try to harm you if you dream of rats. Some superstitions believe that rats contain the souls of men, so their actions should be observed and acted upon.

REBIRTH

Psychological Meaning "On the way of true development, something old must die and something new must be born in him...."—Collins. A dream about rebirth shows that you are entering a new chapter of life. You may have discovered inspiring new goals, values, or a way of expressing your true self. The past is dead. Long live the future!

Mystical Meaning Most spiritual traditions use rebirth symbols or baptism to symbolize the entry into the spiritual life. One of the most beautiful symbols of rebirth is the magnificent phoenix. He is consumed by the fire he brought but is reborn from the ashes. Rebirth can represent spiritual transformation and hope.

RED (SEE COLORS)

REFUGEE

Psychological Meaning Do you feel like an outcast? Perhaps you feel that you have been socially rejected, or the dream represents the way you feel emotionally isolated. Similarly, the dream may highlight your desire to escape or dodge an issue. You will never find security if you keep running away from your problems.

Mystical Meaning Displaced people of any kind indicate that well-conceived plans will fail.

REINCARNATION

Psychological Meaning The dream may be referring to some event in your known past. However, you may also be recalling memories of lives that you have lived before. In the East they believe that memories of past lives will be revealed when the spiritual aspirant has reached a suitable level of inner development. Past lives are then spontaneously recalled during meditation or dreams.

Mystical Meaning Hollywood actor Sylvester Stallone is convinced that he lived during the French Revolution; singer Engelbert Humperdinck believes he was once a Roman emperor; and pop star Tina Turner was told by a Californian psychic that she was the incarnation of a woman pharaoh named Hatshepsut. You are not alone in believing that there are memories of lost lives locked away in the unconscious.

REJECTION (*SEE ALSO* ABANDONMENT)

Psychological Meaning You may be refusing to accept an influence in your life or a situation that is being imposed upon you. If you are the one rejected, it may reveal that you have hidden feelings of a lack of self-worth or alienation from others. Sometimes there are sexual undertones to this type of dream. Freud would say that it is you who are rejecting yourself. Your super-ego (conventional conscience and attitudes) is rejecting your sexual desire. You may be punishing yourself.

Mystical Meaning Some dream oracles insist that you reverse your dream. Rejection therefore means success.

RELATIONSHIPS

Psychological Meaning The people who appear in your dreams, particularly strangers, usually represent facets of yourself. It may be shocking to see the truth about yourself that is projected into the characters of the dream. Your relationships with these people illustrate how much you are in harmony with yourself and demonstrate which parts of your personality you allow to take the stage. For example, if a man dreams of very feminine women, it may show a need to accept the feminine side of his nature. Similarly, a woman who dreams of assertive men may herself need to act in a more masculine way. And, of course, the dream could be talking about real-life scenarios and the true or repressed feelings you have for the people you know in reality.

Mystical Meaning Dream superstition says that the way people act toward you in a dream predicts events to come. If they are friendly, expect happy events to follow. If they are downright nasty, take precautions against potential disaster.

REPAIRING

Psychological Meaning Dreaming of repairing something indicates that you are recovering from something that may have upset you. You are undergoing a period of self-renewal. The item that is being repaired is a symbol of the area of your life or yourself that you are working on.

Mystical Meaning Some people believe that if you dream of sewing the clothes you are wearing it brings terrible bad luck.

RESCUE

Psychological Meaning The person or thing that you rescue may represent an aspect of yourself that has been neglected or ignored. They symbolize an aspect of yourself that is trying to find expression. If you are being rescued, then consider what the scene represents. For example, rescue from a ferocious animal may show that you fear your animal nature. Rescue from a stormy sea may show how close you came to drowning in your emotions. Who is it that rescues you? This person may represent the psychological qualities and attitudes that you should apply to your life.

Mystical Meaning Mystical traditions claim that everyone has the potential to be super human. Deep within you is a psychological resource that enables you to achieve just about anything. You can rescue any situation. Nothing is impossible.

REVOLUTION

Psychological Meaning To dream of taking part in a revolution may represent an inner revolution that is happening to your attitudes and behavior. You no longer need to conform to what society expects of you. You can be yourself.

Mystical Meaning Dreaming of a revolution may spell troubles for business affairs. If blood is spilt it is a sign that you are taking too many financial risks.

REBIRTH

RIDING

Psychological Meaning Freud advises that riding a bicycle, a motorbike, or a horse symbolizes the rhythm of the sexual act. A tame and well-controlled horse may symbolize control of your passions, whereas a runaway horse represents the opposite. The dream could also be a pun. Is your ego "riding high"?

Mystical Meaning This is deemed by superstition to be a very fortunate dream, particularly if someone you love rides with you.

RING

Psychological Meaning The dream may refer to marriage or commitment to a relationship. You may feel that you want to be loyal to your partner. Similarly, a ring could mean loyalty to your principles and ideals. It may represent a binding oath. From a spiritual perspective, a ring, being a circle with no beginning and no end, can represent eternity, wholeness, and your true self.

Mystical Meaning To dream of being given a ring augurs well, but to lose a ring is a warning of trouble. If you dream of finding a ring it means you will soon have a new friend or lover. However, some superstitions say that to dream of being given a ring means a broken promise.

RITUALS

Psychological Meaning Rituals can symbolize the transitions in life. They are also a form of drama that invites you to escape the confines of the conscious mind and pass into the world of the imagination. According to Carl Jung, images of fertility rites in dreams emerge from the collective unconscious in an attempt to abolish the separation between the conscious and unconscious minds. Your dream is putting you in touch with your instinctive self.

Mystical Meaning Shamanic rituals induce a dreamlike state and may trigger clairvoyant and prophetic powers. Make a note of your dream that you can refer to later on, as your dream may include a real prophecy.

RIVER

Psychological Meaning A river may represent the flow of the life force. In a spiritual sense, it may show your acceptance of divine will and destiny. Instead of struggling against life you "go with the flow." Crossing a river may symbolize a fundamental change of lifestyle.

Mystical Meaning Consider your dream in the light of this quotation from *Siddhartha* by Hermann Hesse: "But he learned more from the river than Vasudeva could teach him. He learned from it continually. Above all, he learned from it how to listen with a still heart, with a waiting, open soul, without passion, without desire, without judgment, without opinions."

ROADS

Psychological Meaning Your dream may be a metaphor for the roads you travel through life. The twists, turns, and obstacles are the difficulties you encounter in ordinary life. A fork in the road or a crossroads may represent a difficult decision you have to make.

Mystical Meaning Flowers or trees bordering a road predict success, say the dream books of long ago.

ROBBER

Psychological Meaning You may feel that someone has stolen your success. For example, a work colleague may have accepted the praise and honor for work that is in reality yours. Similarly, you may feel robbed of your ability to express yourself emotionally or act in a decisive way. What is it that has been stolen? This may represent the part of yourself that needs to be recovered from the unconscious.

Mystical Meaning The Gypsies believe that to dream of robbing means that you have a guilty conscience. However, if you dream of being part of a gang of robbers this means that you can count on your friends.

ROBOT

Psychological Meaning This dream may be telling you that you are behaving in a mechanical way and have lost the ability to express feelings. Is your emotional life running on automatic? Do you speak from the heart, or are your responses unnatural and rigid? Similarly, the dream may be portraying your working life. Perhaps work is making you feel like a robot?

Mystical Meaning Erich Von Daniken aside, robots have not featured in traditional mysticism. However, they have become a modern archetype. Why is it that the Daleks, Terminator, and Hal are so frightening? These machines symbolize the fear of losing the sense of humanity in this mechanical age. They can also represent the inevitability of death.

ROCK

Psychological Meaning A rock symbolizes permanence and security. It is the foundation or essence of the self. If you dream of sailing toward rocks, this is a signal that you may be encountering a dangerous situation. Perhaps you should set a different course?

Mystical Meaning The Sirens who lured sailors to their death upon the rocks with their singing are dream symbols for the negative side of the intuition. The dangerous rocks are reminders not to disregard the practical realities of the real world. Idealism should not be taken to extremes.

ROOMS (see also Buildings)

Psychological Meaning Rooms stand for different aspects of your personality. The living room represents the conscious mind; the cellars, the unconscious; and the upper rooms represent your higher aspirations and spirituality.

Mystical Meaning The variations on this theme are too numerous to list. However, one interesting superstition states that to dream of your bedroom means that you will visit faraway lands.

ROSE

Psychological Meaning A red rose has been the traditional symbol of love since Roman times. The theme of your dream is likely to be about love and the way you feel about your past and present emotional relationships. Freud considered the red rose to symbolize the female genitalia, or the blood of menstruation. In addition, the way a flower unfolds and its symmetry are reminiscent of a mandala (see Mandala), which is a symbol of the wholeness of the self.

Mystical Meaning The Romans believed that the rose could protect the dead from evil spirits and so decorated their tombs with the flower. As a dream symbol, it therefore meant safety and protection. Most oracles believe roses to be a favorable omen.

RUBBISH (see Garbage)

RUINS

Psychological Meaning Do you feel that your life is in ruins? Perhaps your business collapsed or a relationship has failed. This dream represents your feeling of defeat. Perhaps this demolition was necessary. You can start again to build a new life.

Mystical Meaning To dream of finding ancient ruins or holy relics may symbolize your discovery of the treasures that lie within you. You are uncovering the ancient wisdom of the unconscious.

RULES (see Police)

SACRIFICE

Psychological Meaning If you are the sacrificial victim, the dream may be a reflection of your attitude. Do you always play the martyr? Perhaps you have tendencies of self-punishment and self-denial. You may feel that other people undervalue your talents and good qualities.

If you are performing the sacrifice, consider what it is you are sacrificing. An animal may represent part of your instinctive nature, or a person you know may represent an aspect of your personality. Perhaps you are sacrificing your principles or your human values? In a spiritual context, the ego must be sacrificed so the divine self can emerge.

Mystical Meaning Ritual sacrifices were a way to appease the gods and bring fertility to the land. The individual was sacrificed for the sake of social and cosmic unity. In Hinduism, Purusha was slain to make men; in Egyptian myth, Osiris is cut to pieces by his brother, Seth; in the Greek stories, Orpheus is torn apart by women; and in Christianity Jesus is crucified. These powerful images of surrender to God still appear in the dreaming life of modern man.

SAFE

Psychological Meaning A safe may be a symbol of the things you hold dear. It may represent the innermost qualities of your true self, the treasure that lies within you. It could also represent a secret. Is there an aspect of your character that you want to hide from the world?

Mystical Meaning Dream oracles are clear about this one. If you dream that you are breaking open a safe, you will not marry the person with whom you are now in love. An empty safe indicates an early marriage and a full one predicts a late marriage.

SAILOR

Psychological Meaning A sailor represents the adventurous side of your personality. It can represent your desire to explore the unknown reaches of the unconscious as symbolized by the sea or may simply represent your desire to travel.

Mystical Meaning As well as the straightforward interpretation of travel, dream oracles advise that dreams of sailors on shore predict a new romance. If they are aboard ships, there will

be news from far away. It is unlucky for a woman to dream of being a sailor.

SAINTS

Psychological Meaning A saint may be a messenger from your higher self to help you to see your situation from a spiritual perspective.

Mystical Meaning For a devout Christian, this dream may be a direct encounter with the spirit of one of the saints who are claimed to help sincere worshipers through dreams. Similarly, in India it is said that a living guru, and also those who have passed into the next life, can help the devotee through dreams. As a spiritualist medium, I believe that advanced souls can use dreams as guides.

SALT

Psychological Meaning Salt can represent the spiritual essence of life. (Salt preserves and is in itself indestructible. It is also the residue that remains after the body has decayed.) It may also represent tears, for these taste of salt, or the unconscious, as symbolized by the sea. Alternatively, your dream may be saying that someone is "rubbing salt in the wound."

Mystical Meaning Salt has also been used as a symbol for enlightenment. If salt is mixed with water, what becomes of it? The salt crystals are gone, but taste the water and you'll know it's still there. It is the same when the self merges with Nirvana. The individual is gone but the essence remains as part of the One.

SAVAGE (SEE ALSO SHADOW)

Psychological Meaning This dream may allude to your sexuality. The savage represents your primitive urges. In addition, the savage may be a shadow figure representing the aspects of yourself that you reject or banish to the jungles of the unconscious.

Mystical Meaning Sometimes the shadow can appear in a helpful guise. For example, in one of the oldest mythical stories in the world, Gilgamesh is helped by the dark Enkidu, lord of the forests. Similar dreamlike images are found in the noble savage, from Aldous Huxley's *Brave New World* (1932) to the story of Mowgli, in Rudyard Kipling's *Jungle Book* (1894).

SCALES

Psychological Meaning Your dream may be helping you make a decision. You are weighing the pros and cons of a situation. It may also be telling you that you need to take a balanced view of a situation and not get so emotional. If you are interested in astrology, scales may represent the zodiacal sign Libra; this may be a Libra you know or may become the characteristics of this sign that you exhibit.

Mystical Meaning Since ancient times, scales have been a symbol of Justice. Ancient Egyptian images show that the soul is weighed in the scales of Justice by the jackal-headed god Anubis. Your dream may be saying that justice will be done.

Common Dream

SCHOOL (SEE ALSO EXAMINATION)

I am now in my 70s, yet last night I dreamed that I was back at my childhood school. In the dream the teacher scolds me, and I notice that the classroom is in a state of decay.—Gary T, Leeds, England

Psychological Meaning Dreams set at school are very often reported by people from all age groups. Sometimes these dreams highlight childhood insecurities that have still not been resolved. For example, this dream, set in a decaying school building, suggests that the dreamer is carrying disappointed childhood expectations or unpleasant memories. In addition, the schoolteacher is a classic symbol for authority and may represent his father and others who have determined the course of his life. The schoolteacher may also represent the censoring aspect of his personality that keeps the chaotic impulses in control. Being scolded may indicate that the dreamer has feelings of guilt or inferiority or that he worries that his misdeeds will be found out. Alternatively, if the teacher in the dream were praising Gary, it would indicate that Gary had self-confidence and believed in his own abilities.

Another interpretation of dreams set at school is as a metaphor for what you are learning from life over a long period. These dreams may also carry a feeling of nostalgia and reveal a hidden desire to recapture the freedom, optimism, and ambition of these formative years.

ASK YOURSELF

1. *Do I have any unresolved anxieties from my childhood?* Clearly these problems are not going to be solved overnight, but your dream may be helping you come to terms with long-standing worries that need to be addressed. Becoming aware of and identifying your anxieties is the first step in the healing process.

2. *Does the dream teach me a lesson?* The dream may be showing you what you can learn from your circumstances today. Life itself is like a school, and there are many tests. I like to think that God gives his hardest lessons to his best pupils. It may explain why the most deserving people often have the most wretched lives.

Mystical Meaning Some dream superstitions claim that to dream of teaching at school is a sign of good fortune. However, you will experience setbacks in business if you dream of being a pupil. These will be particularly bad if you dream of forgetting your lessons.

SCISSORS (SEE ALSO CUTTING)

Psychological Meaning Precise cutting indicates control and decisiveness in your waking life.

Mystical Meaning Dreams of scissors are usually interpreted by superstition dream lore to indicate that an enemy will do you harm. However, if they are clean and bright you have nothing to fear.

SEA (SEE ALSO WATER)

Psychological Meaning The sea may represent the unconscious, and your dream may show that you are now ready to explore the intuitive and instinctive aspects of yourself. Sailing on a boat or putting out to sea may represent this journey into the unknown part of you. (For a man this can represent the search for the feminine side of his nature.) The condition of the sea may depict the way you are feeling. For example, a stormy sea may indicate that you feel angry about something or threatened by forces outside your control. However, a calm sea may show inner contentment and peace of mind. Freud considered the sea and the incoming tide to be symbols of sexual union.

Mystical Meaning In primal myths, the sea existed before the creation of humanity and is therefore like a womb from which the rest of creation emerges. In the legends, the creator god wrestles with the sea goddess, who is impregnated to give birth to the world. The sea is therefore a symbol of the raw materials of existence and is associated with the creative potential of your true self. From a spiritual perspective, the sea may represent the totality of existence. It is the ultimate reality, the One of which we are all a part. Enlightenment is gained when the individual self merges with the infinite. This exalted state of consciousness is likened to a raindrop merging with the sea.

SEARCHING

Psychological Meaning What are you trying to find? Your dream search may symbolize the quest to find something physical, emotional, intellectual, or spiritual. You may be searching for a new way to solve an old problem. If you dream of searching for someone you know, you may be anxious about your relationship with that person and may want to end the emotional separation. Are you sure that this search is worthwhile, or is the dream reflecting your feeling of hopelessness?

Mystical Meaning Perhaps your dream is a spiritual search. Myths such as the quest for the Holy Grail by King Arthur's knights may be describing the inner process of spiritual transformation.

SEASONS

Psychological Meaning The seasons can represent your state of mind and prevailing psychological or material conditions. They remind you that everything is subject to change and renewal.

Here are the meanings for Northern Hemisphere countries:

Spring: Optimism and rebirth are associated with springtime. Spring may represent a new beginning for you or new projects and a new attitude toward life. It may represent youth.

Summer: Pleasure and happiness are associated with summertime, as are relaxation and vacations. It may symbolize early middle age.

Autumn: This time may represent a maturing of your ideas. It is also a time for preparation and the ending of a cycle. It is a time when the trees bear fruit, and so may represent the fruition of a plan. Autumn may symbolize late middle age.

Winter: A time of rest, but your dream may be expressing feelings that your life is barren and empty. It may symbolize old age.

Mystical Meaning The movement of the sun across the sky, the solstices, and the seasons since earliest times have come to represent the phases of human life. They also relate to the four elements: the bare earth, to winter; rain, to spring; heat and fire, to summer; and the element of air, to the winds of fall.

SEED

Psychological Meaning A seed is a symbol of potential. It may show that you have recognized an opportunity in your waking life or it may represent your potential for personal growth. For a couple planning a family, it may represent conception.

Mystical Meaning My research reveals that seeds represent increasing prosperity in most archaic dream books.

SEVEN (SEE NUMBERS)

SEX

Psychological Meaning Erotic dreams are usually a straightforward expression of sexual desire. The nature of the sex may reveal your hidden hopes and fears. For example, if you dream of having sex with someone other than your partner, it may highlight dissatisfaction with the physical side of your relationship. Your dreams may reveal patterns in your sexual relationships that you may not be aware of. If your sexual dreams are violent or perverse, you may need to be more relaxed about your sexuality. You may have sexual phobias or compulsions that need to

SEX

be recognized and brought under control. Your dreams may offer ways to help you lead a happier and more natural sexual life.

Mystical Meaning An odd superstition claims that if a man or woman dreams of visiting a brothel, there will be an improvement to domestic life. And good news for cross-dressers: there will be success within the family if you dream of changing sex.

SHADOW

Psychological Meaning The "shadow" is the dark side of your nature. It represents everything you wish not to be. It is also the unused or rejected side of yourself and your emotions. It is your dark side that you refuse to recognize. It is the repressed aspects of the self. Try to bring these hidden feelings into the light of day so that they loosen their hold over you, otherwise you are likely to project this "other self" on to other people. Do you accuse others of faults that are, in reality, your own?

Mystical Meaning Many superstitions say that the "shadow" is a part of a person's soul. To tread on it or throw stones at it is unlucky and may cause a person harm. Beware if you dream that this happens to you.

SHAPES (SEE NUMBERS AND MANDALA)

SHEEP (SEE ALSO LAMB)

Psychological Meaning Are you being a conformist? To dream of sheep may indicate that you are following a conventional way and falling in with what everyone expects of you. Perhaps you should try a less orthodox approach to your situation. Why keep following the flock? The opposite meaning is symbolized by the ram, which is an individualist. Similarly, to dream of a shepherd may represent the power of love that can unify divergent tendencies. This may apply to your world or the conflicts within yourself.

Mystical Meaning Consider this quote from the Vedas: "Come up, Lions, and shake off the delusion that you are sheep. You are souls immortal, spirits free, blest, and eternal. Ye are not matter; ye are not bodies; matter is your servant, not you the servant of matter." Also associated with the

Christian "lamb of God," sheep are considered to be a lucky dream omen.

SHELLS

Psychological Meaning Shells are usually a spiritual symbol because they come from the sea, which represents the vast expanses of the unconscious mind. They are also a divine feminine symbol associated with the goddess Venus, who was born from a shell. (The shape of a shell is reminiscent of the vagina, say Freudian psychologists.) A heavy tortoise shell may represent your desire for protection. Similarly, a delicate eggshell may symbolize your feelings of vulnerability. Finally, eggshells can represents thin-skinned egotism which, like the arrogant Humpty Dumpty, is easily smashed to pieces.

Mystical Meaning According to some authorities on dream superstition, shells predict that something strange will happen to you. So if you wake to find you've been abducted by aliens or there's a flipper where your foot was, it is probably the shell dream that's to blame.

SHIP

Psychological Meaning A ship may represent the course of your life, and the type of ship may say something about your state of mind. For example, you may be in a pleasant mood when you dream about a cruise ship but may be feeling aggressive if it's a warship. A lifeboat may represent your need to be rescued from the stormy emotions and troubles that beset you, and traveling on a submarine may show your desire to explore the unconscious. Or perhaps the dream is simply encouraging about your material success by saying that your ship's come in.

Mystical Meaning A ship in dock or on a calm sea is claimed by the ancient seers to promise happiness in love. If there are storms, happiness will be delayed. There will be worrying news if you dream of a shipwreck.

SHIRT

Psychological Meaning This dream may represent your self-image and the way you present yourself to the world. A starched shirt may symbolize formal conservatism, whereas a bright or

SHADOW

unbuttoned shirt may show your unconventional free spirit.

Mystical Meaning The Gypsies believe that the more colorful the shirt you dream of, the luckier you will be.

SHOES

Psychological Meaning Freud proposed that items of clothing that can be entered by parts of the body are sexual symbols. Fairy tales often use the same language of symbols as are found in dreams. When Cinderella put her foot into the shoe, it was a symbol of her desire for sexual relations with the prince.

Mystical Meaning Superstition says that to dream of losing a shoe predicts an illness. This may originate from an old English rural superstition that says that burning a smelly old shoe in the home helps avoid infection in the house. Dusty shoes indicate an unexpected journey, and shiny ones mean happiness in love.

SHOOTING

Psychological Meaning Freud says that guns represent male sexuality, and shooting a gun is a symbol for ejaculation. This may also be saying that your plans are right on target and that you know what you are aiming for in life.

Mystical Meaning If you dream of enjoying the shoot, there will be good fortune, but if you are filled with fear there will be difficulties. Shooting stars are universally regarded as good luck and their appearance in dreams is auspicious.

SHOP

Psychological Meaning Shops can symbolize the array of opportunities and rewards that life offers. However, if you dream that the shop is closed or that you have insufficient money, this indicates that you feel the things you want from life are unattainable. Your dream may be telling you to lower your expectations and set yourself goals that are more realistic.

Mystical Meaning To a tradesman this is an unlucky dream signifying many pressing creditors. For everyone else it is an omen of prosperity, so long as you don't buy anything. You will be blessed with good fortune if you dream of working in a shop.

SHORE

Psychological Meaning As a dream symbol the shore is the place where the conscious mind meets the unconscious. The dream may also represent a journey, either an actual one or the symbolic journey of self-discovery across the sea of the unconscious.

Mystical Meaning Some authorities claim that an empty beach is a sign of opportunity. Dream of a busy beach, and you will soon feel secure.

SHOWER

Psychological Meaning A shower may symbolize spiritual energy and cleansing. You have been cleansed, your worries are washed away, and you can begin afresh.

Mystical Meaning A shower may be a symbol of healing. Here's a healing technique you can try: Stand upright and imagine that a shower of liquid light is pouring from above. It washes over you and through you. As it does, it washes away all illness, pain, and worries and replaces these dark spots with glorious, shining light. Now fill yourself with light from your toes to the top of your head. Your dream may have given you a clue to self-healing. Now try it in waking life.

SIGNPOST (SEE ALSO CITY AND CROSSROADS)

Psychological Meaning Many dreams are about problem-solving. Your dream is showing you the direction to take in life. What is the destination the sign suggests? The name of the town it points to may be a pun to represent the human qualities you need.

Mystical Meaning The Gypsies say that to dream of a wooden or stone signpost indicates that you will soon be able to say goodbye to a period of indecision.

SILVER

Psychological Meaning Silver represents something you value. This may be something such as your financial needs or your own inner emotional resources. There may be an allusion to the moon and therefore to the feminine qualities of intuition and feeling.

Mystical Meaning To dream that you have silver in your purse is a sign that you will lose money. It is not considered a lucky metal to dream about.

SINGING

Psychological Meaning Your dream is expressing your current feelings. The nature of the music and the words of the song may say something about you and your situation.

Mystical Meaning Singing can be an expression of spirituality. Consider your dream in light of this quote from Rabindranath Tagore: "God respects me when I work, but he loves me when I sing."

SINKING (SEE ALSO DROWNING)

Psychological Meaning You may fear being overwhelmed by your emotions or worries about a situation. You may fear that something of importance in your life is ending. For example, you may be concerned about a failing relationship or business enterprise. It could be a symbol of despair. You have a choice: sink or swim.

Mystical Meaning An acclaimed astrologer and phrenologist claims that this dream means you've been spending too much money shopping!

SISTER (SEE ALSO SHADOW, ANIMA/ANIMUS)

Psychological Meaning Carl Jung claimed that childhood sibling rivalry and jealousy influence the dream symbol of the sister. For a female dreamer, she may represent the shadow side of the personality that is neglected and undeveloped. Sometimes this may include anti-social qualities that are alarming. However, in a man's dreams a sister may represent the female side of his own personality (anima).

Mystical Meaning A sister may occur as a guide in a man's dreams and take him into a dark forest, into the depths of the earth, or to the bottom of the sea. This theme, which occurs in many myths and legends, shows that the anima can guide the ego to the cause of a psychological difficulty.

SITTING

Psychological Meaning Your dream may indicate that you are taking a passive position about something. Perhaps your inaction is causing problems. Instead of "sitting on the fence," you may need to act.

Mystical Meaning If you dream of sitting on a high seat, your luck will be good, but if the seat is low, expect disappointments.

SKELETON (SEE BONES)

SKIN

Psychological Meaning Skin is the outermost part of yourself. Your dream may be saying something about the way you present yourself to others. A skin rash may be a play on words, indicating that you are making a rash decision. Or it may simply highlight your worries about your physical appearance. Perhaps you don't like to show your emotions. Are you thick-skinned?

Mystical Meaning The Baluchi women of Oman believe that to dream of pale skin indicates that a person will receive many jewels.

SKULL (SEE ALSO BONES)

Psychological Meaning Carl Jung decided to become a psychologist after dreaming of discovering a skull in a deep cellar under his house. The skull represented his desire to probe the secrets of the mind. To dream of a skull may also symbolize mortality and your spiritual contemplation of the meaning of life and death. It may also refer to finality and the things in life that cannot be avoided.

Mystical Meaning To the Gypsies, a skull represents wisdom derived from their ancestors. To drink from a skull means sharing in their wisdom. In Ireland, it can be a symbol of truth, for it is believed that if a man takes an oath on a skull but is lying, he will die soon after.

SKY

Psychological Meaning If the sky is a dominant image in your dream, you may be thinking about the spiritual meaning of life and the purpose of human existence. The daytime sky represents cosmic consciousness, as opposed to ordinary awareness. It is usually associated with God. A star-studded night sky may represent the world of the unconscious. Jung saw the night sky as the most suitable place for man to project unconscious content. The symbolism of the constellations and the zodiacal signs are archetypal expressions of the inner world of the unconscious.

Mystical Meaning Most dream superstitions agree that to dream of a blue sky brings good luck, but cloudy skies spell misfortune. Some authorities claim that to dream of a red sky forecasts that a terrible disaster will befall the nation.

SLEEPING

Psychological Meaning Dreaming of being asleep may indicate that part of you needs to be jazzed up a bit. You may have become complacent or dull. From a philosophical standpoint, it may represent the nature of the human predicament. Ignorance is sleep, but to understand reality you have to awaken.

Mystical Meaning Many people report dreaming of seeing themselves asleep in bed. When it first happened to me I suddenly realized that I was actually standing outside my body. This phenomenon is known as astral traveling.

SMELL

Psychological Meaning Perfumers realize that smells trigger emotional reactions. They compose a fragrance like a piece of music, with high, middle, and low notes. What emotions are created by smells in your dream? If you feel disgust, you may be reacting again to aspects of your own nature or to the attitudes of others. Perhaps you had an argument and are still fuming, or something about your situation makes you "smell a rat"?

Mystical Meaning Each smell has a specific meaning. Here are some examples: camphor, scandal; ginger, a love affair; jasmine, a true spiritual experience; lavender, a happy relationship; nutmeg, deceit.

SMILE

Psychological Meaning Your dream may be expressing your approval of decisions you have made. You may feel pleased with your successes and achievements. There is a promise of happiness. Enjoy this nice, smug feeling.

Mystical Meaning Perhaps your dream is telling you to cheer up a bit. The Indian guru Paramahansa Yogananda in his book *Man's Eternal Quest* encourages his followers to be smile millionaires: "My smile comes from a joy deep within my being, a joy that you also may attain. Like a fragrance, it oozes out from the core of the blossoming soul. This joy calls others to bathe in its waters of divine bliss."

SMOKE

Psychological Meaning Smoke is caused when a fire is stifled. Ask yourself what part of your self needs to come to expression. Let your true self shine.

Mystical Meaning A bad omen. Smoke brings disappointment unless you dream that it annoys you.

SNAKES

Psychological Meaning The snake is one of the world's oldest symbols, found in some of the most ancient sculptures. Snakes are often used

---

FAMOUS DREAMER

Abraham Lincoln
U.S. president (1809 – 1865)

Abraham Lincoln dreamed he heard weeping coming from the East Room of the White House. He walked into the room and was shocked to realize he had interrupted a funeral service. In front of him was a corpse wrapped in funeral vestment and laid on a catafalque. It was guarded by soldiers and surrounded by a large crowd of mourners.

"Who is dead?" Lincoln asked one of the guards.

"The president," came the reply. "He was assassinated."

The weeping and wailing of the crowd became so loud that Lincoln awoke. He spent the rest of the night pale-faced as he contemplated the hidden meaning of his dream.

Abraham Lincoln died on April 15, 1865, the morning after being shot by John Wilkes Booth in a box at Ford's Theater, in Washington, D.C.

as phallic symbols and have long been linked with pagan fertility gods. Because it lives close to the ground, the snake is an emblem of the nurturing earth and also the unknown perils of the underworld. Christian imagery emphasizes the dark side of this symbol. It is considered evil, yet it is the snake, created by God, that tempts man to gain knowledge. In dreams, a snake can represent hidden fears. Falling into a pit of snakes may represent the many worries that are threatening you. Sometimes snakes can symbolize the poisonous words and innuendo of the people around you.

Mystical Meaning Entwined snakes appear on the god Mercury's caduceus, which is the symbol of the medical profession to this day. The Greeks attributed healing powers to the snake. Similar symbolism may be found in Indian Kundalini yoga, where it represents the life force that rises up the spinal chord. In particular, the cobra is a symbol of divine enlightenment and is associated with the god Shiva.

SNOW (SEE ALSO ICE)

Psychological Meaning Snow can indicate frozen emotions but can also symbolize transformation and purification. Clean, pure snow can represent a fresh start. Melting snow can indicate that obstacles and fears are dissolving, whereas an avalanche of snow can indicate that you fear being overwhelmed by emotions that have been held in check for too long. Are you cold and lacking warmth?

Mystical Meaning To dream of watching falling snow indicates that a letter will arrive shortly. Some superstitions claim it will be from the person you will marry. The truth is that most oracles consider this dream to be one of good luck.

SOLDIER

Psychological Meaning Associated with aggression and conquest, a soldier may represent the way you impose your feelings on others. You may be preparing to do battle over an issue in your waking life or may feel the need to defend yourself from an emotional attack. Be careful how you use your power.

Mystical Meaning For a man, this dream means a change at work. For a woman, it's a warning about a casual relationship. Some oracles believe it means a lawsuit, whereas the Gypsies say you will soon receive honors.

SON

Psychological Meaning A son may represent the youthful part of yourself. He may also represent your own potential. Perhaps you recognize in him the ideal and hopes that you once had. The son may of course have no symbolic meaning at all, and the dream may simply be about your own son. Are you worried about him?

Mystical Meaning According to superstition, it is fortunate to dream about your son. If you dream he is getting married, there'll be family worries.

SONG (SEE MUSIC)

SOUNDS (SEE ALSO MUSIC, FLYING)

Psychological Meaning Loud sounds can indicate that the unconscious is trying to draw your attention to an issue. A bugle being blown may show a call to arms, suggesting that you must become more alert to problems of pressing importance. A whistle may indicate that someone has exposed your clandestine plans ("blown the whistle") or it can show that you are being obedient, like a dog responding to its master's call. To hear muffled or indistinct voices indicates that you must listen more carefully to your wise inner voice. Sometimes dreams incorporate sounds such as the alarm clock or traffic outside your bedroom into the dream and weave them into the symbolism of the dream.

Mystical Meaning If the subtle body re-enters the physical body too quickly after an out-of-body experience, the dreamer may hear a loud crack, like a shotgun being fired in the room. This is very disconcerting but quite normal. It will disappear once you master the art of astral travel.

SPIDER

Psychological Meaning A spider may represent a fear. Perhaps you feel trapped in a web of deceit or entangled by emotions and fears from which you cannot escape? Alternatively, are you the spider that's spinning a web to ensnare someone else? Sigmund Freud believed that in dreams spiders represent the devouring mother who consumes her children through possessiveness or her power to arouse guilt. She is symbolized by the spider that traps and lives off her innocent victims. (Freud's mother has a lot to answer for!)

Mystical Meaning Arachnophobia may be an instinctive fear that originates from primordial times when poisonous spiders were common. Your dream draws upon these ancient memories to express the fear you have about something that is upsetting you. Superstitions dating back to the Middle Ages claim that it is lucky to dream of spiders.

SPIRAL

Psychological Meaning An upward spiral may represent advancement and progress. A downward spiral may represent despair and failure. Are things spiraling out of control?

Mystical Meaning According to the Chinese mystical tradition of *feng shui*, spirals are very auspicious symbols that stimulate health, wealth, and happiness. *Chi* energy, the life force, is said to be at its best when it moves in spirals.

SPIRITS (SEE GHOST)

SPIT

Psychological Meaning You may wish to be rid of something that is part of yourself. Perhaps you feel the need for inner cleansing and spiritual healing. Spitting may represent anger and contempt.

Mystical Meaning Superstitious people agree that if you have a bad dream you can rid yourself of any bad luck by simply spitting three times as soon as you wake up. Please note, this technique can also cause problems in relationships.

STAGE (SEE THEATER)

STARS

Psychological Meaning Stars can represent your higher states of consciousness, the exalted spiritual state that you wish to attain. They can also represent your desire for worldly success, particularly if you work in show biz! Stars may also symbolize the forces of destiny that you feel may be controlling your life at this time. Usually the stars carry a happy, favorable meaning.

Mystical Meaning The ancients believed that when a great person died, he became a star in the sky. To dream of the stars therefore implied that the spirits were guiding you. "Have patience, Candidate, as one who fears no failure, courts no success. Fix thy soul's gaze upon the star whose ray thou art, the flaming star that shines within the lightless depths of ever-being."—Blavatsky

STATION (SEE ALSO TRAIN AND JOURNEY)

Psychological Meaning A station is a point of departure. It indicates that new opportunities await you and that you are preparing for a new

---

FAMOUS DREAMER

Graham Greene
Author

Famous novelist Graham Greene got much of his inspiration from dreams. Some of Greene's dreams contained prophecies, and his diary shows that he foresaw the sinking of the Titanic. He said: "On the April night of the Titanic disaster, when I was five, I dreamt of a shipwreck. One image of the dream has remained with me for more than 60 years: a man in oilskins bent double beside a companion—way under the blow of a great wave."

At least 19 other cases of precognition through dreams and visions have been associated with the sinking of April 14, 1912. For example, London businessman J. Connon Middleton sold his tickets just before the trip because for two nights in a row he dreamed that the Titanic would sink.

and perhaps exciting venture. Railway lines run in straight lines, so your journey to your goal will be direct and on target. A station is also a public place, so it may represent your role in society.

Mystical Meaning It is fortunate to dream of meeting someone at the station, for this means that your career will be helped forward by someone with great influence. It can also signify news coming.

STATUE

Psychological Meaning A statue or bust often represents the desire to idealize someone or something. If you do this and put the person on a pedestal, you only increase the perceived feeling of remoteness and unattainability associated with this person or situation.

Mystical Meaning If you dream of a statue coming alive, it means that you will reform a broken friendship. Some oracles deem sculptors to be auspicious omens. If you see one working or dream of being one, your fortunes will change for the better.

STEALING

Psychological Meaning Do you feel that someone has cheated you, or perhaps it is you who have been less than honest? You may unconsciously feel that you have set your sights too high and feel that you cannot attain your goal without breaking the rules. The dream could also represent needs that are not being met and a lack of fulfillment.

Mystical Meaning Some superstitions say that this dream refers to matters of the heart. You may be infatuated with someone.

STICK

Psychological Meaning A stick may be an instrument of punishment or power. If you are punishing an animal with a stick, you may have negative feelings toward your instinctive nature. The people you hit with a stick may represent the part of yourself that you are in conflict with. Freud on this one: the stick is a phallic symbol.

Mystical Meaning Masters of mystical oneiromancy (predicting the future through dreams) say that to dream of sticks is an unlucky omen.

STONE

Psychological Meaning Stone can represent permanence and the things that endure. Similarly, it can represent the unchanging eternal self. However, it can also symbolize coldness, stubbornness, and a refusal to change. Perhaps it represents a weighty problem that you have to deal with?

Mystical Meaning Stones on the road symbolize awkward people who stop your progress; throwing stones indicates accusations; and some oracles say that if you dream of collecting stones you'll inherit some land. Finding precious stones is of course a symbol of good luck.

STORM

Psychological Meaning A storm may indicate emotional conflict or turmoil within you. It may indicate anger or frustration that lacks an outlet.

Mystical Meaning Superstition says that this is an obstacle dream that indicates separation from what you desire. If your house is damaged by a storm, people with evil intention are nearby.

STORY (SEE ALSO BUILDINGS AND HOUSE)

Psychological Meaning The stories of a building represent levels of consciousness. The top floor may represent your spirituality, and the basement represents the unconscious. The floors in between represent the many states of mind that you experience.

Mystical Meaning If you dream of being at the top of a big building, you will achieve success.

STRANGER (SEE ALSO SHADOW)

Psychological Meaning A stranger represents those aspects of yourself that you either reject or are unfamiliar with. Are there aspects of your personality that you deny? If the stranger is frightening, he may symbolize things you have repressed.

Mystical Meaning Superstition claims that to dream of talking to a stranger means you will hear news from afar. Some oracles claim that this is a dream of contrary meaning that indicates that friends will help you.

STRANGULATION

Psychological Meaning If you dream of being strangled, it may represent something in your life that you feel is emotionally restrictive. To dream of strangling someone may express your frustrations with that person in real life. Alternatively, the person being strangled may represent an aspect of yourself that you are not allowing to be expressed.

Mystical Meaning The dream seers claim that if you make a wish after waking from a dream about strangling someone, the wish will come true.

STREET (SEE ROADS)

STRUGGLE

Psychological Meaning This dream may represent the frustration you feel about your circumstances or an inner conflict of some kind.

Mystical Meaning Your dream may be expressing something about the nature of struggle. Sathya Sai Baba explains: "There is no struggle; only the karmic pattern of the past, which has created apparent problems for the present and future..... Let the love flow and surrender everything to God. Then all your worries, fears, frustrations, doubts, and struggles will fade away. They are all aspects of illusion."

SUFFOCATION (SEE ALSO DROWNING)

Psychological Meaning This dream may indicate that you feel emotionally overwhelmed by a situation that causes you anxiety. You may feel unable to cope. Similarly, you may feel that an emotionally overbearing partner or parent is stifling your psychological growth. It is important that you re-establish your sense of self-identity.

Mystical Meaning Dream superstition says that this dream is a warning about sorrow and ill health.

SUICIDE

Psychological Meaning You are turning your feelings of aggression against yourself. Perhaps you are unable to overcome feelings of guilt or feel degraded and helpless. You may feel unable to cope with a problem that has troubled you for some time. Part of you is crying out for help. I suggest that you talk over your problems with someone you can trust. A problem shared is a problem halved.

Mystical Meaning A dream of disappointment, say the dream oracles.

SUIT (SEE ALSO CLOTHES)

Psychological Meaning A suit may represent your desire to impress someone. It may represent the confident side of your personality or the aspect of your self that you display at work. Perhaps the suit is a pun for "following suit" or being "well suited" to someone.

Mystical Meaning The Gypsies say that to dream of wearing a suit foretells success.

SUMMER (SEE SEASONS)

SUN (SEE ALSO MOON)

Psychological Meaning The sun is a masculine symbol. It is the conscious mind and the intellect. It can be a symbol of the true self and may represent intelligence, as distinct from intuition. A sunrise may indicate a new beginning, whereas a sunset may show the end of a phase. If the sun in your dream is scorching hot, it may indicate that your intellectual powers are dominating the psyche and are in danger of destroying your emotional life.

Mystical Meaning Mankind's first god was the Sun. It drove away the darkness and with it the perils of the night. Invariably it has been considered a symbol of blessing. In the Tarot cards, the sun card represents joy and exuberance. Dream lore generally says the same: to dream of the sun promises happy times ahead.

SWAN

Psychological Meaning A swan is a beautiful, elegant, and calm bird. Your dream may be saying that the right way to behave is with dignity and grace.

Mystical Meaning A swan, with its long neck, may also be a phallic symbol. In the Greek myths, Zeus loved Leda, wife of Tyndareus, King of Sparta, and seduced her by transforming into a swan.

SWEEPING

Psychological Meaning You are getting rid of old ideas and attitudes. Sweep away the junk from the past and open a new and better phase for the future.

Mystical Meaning Superstition says that it is unlucky to sweep waste out of the house, as you may sweep your good luck with it. Dreams of sweeping can have similar negative connotations.

SWIMMING

Psychological Meaning Expanses of water usually symbolize the unconscious. To dream of swimming shows that you trust the unconscious and are supported by it. You have confidence and are receptive to its creative power. If you dream of swimming underwater, it may indicate that you have accepted and are at one with your unconscious. This union is even more apparent if you dream of being able to breathe underwater.

Mystical Meaning Swimming strongly in clear water means you will achieve great success in love and business. The opposite applies if you struggle or the water is dirty.

SWORD

Psychological Meaning A sword can represent aggression, but also discrimination, truth, and justice. Attacking someone with a sword may indicate hostility toward that person or what he or she represents, and being stabbed represents your feeling that you've been defeated over something. A sword can also be a phallic symbol.

Mystical Meaning As a symbol of truth, the sword is your consciousness that frees itself from the "devouring mother" aspect of the unconscious. This symbol for the process of individuation often occurs in myths and stories in which the hero slays the dragon or demon with his sword.

SYRUP

Psychological Meaning Are you exhibiting sickly sweet emotions? Syrup may represent excessive sentimentality or nostalgia.

Mystical Meaning Some superstitions associate dreaming of sweet things as sexy. It is now known that the human brain produces a chemical called phenylethylamine when lovers are in a state of excitement. It is also found in chocolate.

TABLE

Psychological Meaning At home and at work people meet and discuss plans over a table. In your dream, it represents your relationships with other people. Items put onto the table represent something about your life that is being brought into the open. Perhaps the dream is saying that you should be more open with people. Perhaps you should "put your cards on the table."

Mystical Meaning A table is an omen of domestic comfort and a happy, contented marriage partner.

TAIL

Psychological Meaning If you dream of growing a tail, it may represent your animal nature. Since the tail is behind you, it may refer to a rejection of the sexual side of yourself.

Mystical Meaning To dream of cutting off the tail of an animal foretells that you will be careless, say the oracles.

TAMING

Psychological Meaning If you dream of taming a wild animal, it may show that you are getting your emotions under control.

Mystical Meaning If you dream of taming a lion, you will be successful in everything you do. Some oracles claim it means you will marry a very intelligent person.

TATTOO

Psychological Meaning The dream may be about emotional situations that have affected you. They've left their mark. It may also be referring to a behavior pattern that has become ingrained into your personality.

Mystical Meaning Your dream may be of a sexual nature. "Tattoo" is a Maori word, and until recently tattooing was accepted in most parts of Polynesia as the ultimate beauty treatment. Many Polynesians had every part of the body done, except the eyes. In many cultures, it is seen as a symbol of sexuality and virility. The inhabitants of the Marquesas consider a tattooed tongue supremely erotic.

TEACHER (*SEE* **SCHOOL**)

TEETH

I dreamed that my teeth were falling out. In real life, my teeth are perfectly all right even though I'm 39 years old. Why should I have this dream?—Katie P., New Orleans, Louisiana

Psychological Meaning Dreaming of teeth falling out may represent insecurity. These dreams often occur at a time of transition between one phase of life and another. When you lost your milk teeth, you also gradually lost your childhood innocence. Losing your teeth therefore shows that today you have similar feelings of uncertainty and self-consciousness as you did in childhood. The dream could also highlight your worries about getting older or your sexual attractiveness.

Animal teeth may represent aggressiveness, and false teeth may represent concern about your self-image. The dream could also be triggered by subtle toothache that you are not yet consciously aware of.

ASK YOURSELF

1. *Do I feel insecure because I'm starting a new phase of life?* Katie's dream may highlight her worries about soon reaching 40.

2. *Am I facing reality?* Dreams about losing teeth may represent a retreat to the innocent times when you were a toothless baby and dependent for nourishment on your mother's milk.

Mystical Meaning The Nilotes of the Sudan believe that if a woman has a toothy grin it is a bad omen. It symbolizes the mouth of a wild animal, which will frighten the cattle. Superstitious lore insists that maidens with a wide smile be made beautiful by having their front teeth removed. An African witch doctor would therefore interpret dreams about losing teeth as a sign of prosperity.

TELEPHONE

Psychological Meaning To dream of a telephone ringing may be your unconscious trying to get your attention. What you hear through the phone is a message from your unconscious. The content of the message may reveal a great deal about your hopes and fears. You may be facing up to issues you have previously avoided.

Mystical Meaning Many people believe that to dream of receiving a telephone call is lucky, for it brings advantages in business. However, if you dream of making a call, there will be postponement of a date. All long-distance calls are said to bring happiness.

TELEVISION (*SEE ALSO* FILM)

Psychological Meaning A television may represent your mind with its flow of thoughts. You are objectively viewing yourself. What is it that moves across this screen of your consciousness? Is your head filled with interesting information or just a lot of mindless soap operas? The programs you dream of watching are an intimate yet objective representation of the things that play on your mind.

Mystical Meaning Modern dream superstition say that if you enjoy dreaming about watching

FAMOUS DREAMER

Julius Caesar
Roman emperor

Nineteen centuries before Freud, the night before Julius Caesar led his army across the Rubicon River to attack Rome, he dreamed that he slept with his mother. Caesar interpreted this dream to mean that the invasion would succeed.

Unfortunately, he later failed to heed the dream warning of his wife, Calpurnia, who warned him to "beware the Ides of March." On March 15th, in 44 B.C., Caesar was assassinated in the Senate by republicans, including Brutus and Cassius, who feared his monarchical aspirations.

television you will achieve success, but if you are upset by what you see, you will be led astray by others.

TEMPLE (*see* Church)

TEST (*see* Examination)

THEATER

Psychological Meaning Dreams are themselves like a theater in which your problems, hopes, and fears are acted out by characters generated by your incredible imagination. To dream of a theater is therefore like a dream within a dream. Consequently, these dreams are often lucid because the dream symbolism helps the dreamer realize that he is dreaming. If you dream of watching or acting in a play, pantomime, or circus, consider what aspect of your personality each character represents. You are seeing your life and the way you behave from a new perspective. The dream performance will give you insight into the way you behave and the way you present yourself to the world.

Mystical Meaning Sages who have reached an exulted level of consciousness often point out that life is like theater. You play a part for a short time in a cosmic game. When you die, you take off the costume and return to your true identity. A curious superstition claims that if you dream you cut new teeth, it is a sign you will hear of the birth of a child who will do great things in the theater.

THREAT

Psychological Meaning If you dream of threatening someone, it may represent your need to assert yourself in real life. However, if you are being threatened, you need to determine the cause of this feeling. Some dreams may have an overall menacing atmosphere, and it is hard to determine the cause of this anxiety. These threatening dreams fascinated the Surrealist painters.

It is most likely that your dream is caused by problems in your relationships. You may feel emotionally threatened by a partner, or perhaps you worry about the threat of redundancy or a management change at the workplace. Similarly, inner emotions can threaten your emotional equi-

librium. You may have repressed emotions, such as resentment, anger, eroticism, or fear, that are trying to find a way to be expressed.

Mystical Meaning Some oracles consider this to be a contrary dream. Everyone is going to be sweet and nice to you.

THREE (*see* Numbers)

THUNDER

Psychological Meaning Thunder may represent your feelings of anger. You may have had or be planning an argument. Your relationships may be stormy.

Mystical Meaning The Ancient Greeks believed that storms were caused when Zeus quarreled with his consort, Hera. In the Sumerian mythology that may date from Neolithic times, the storm was associated with the roar of the bull and fertility rites. Your dream may represent the untamed and hugely powerful forces within the psyche.

TICKET (*see also* Key)

Psychological Meaning A ticket may represent the start of a series of psychological events. You may have given yourself permission to begin your exploration of the unconscious. Similarly, the ticket may symbolize your approval to start a new project. You may have decided the direction in which you would like to take your life. If you dream of losing your ticket, you are uncertain about what direction your life is taking and may feel confused about what to do. You may feel psychologically unprepared to deal with an issue from your waking life.

Mystical Meaning You will receive some news that will clarify your position.

TIGER

Psychological Meaning A tiger may symbolize something that frightens you. It may represent repressed feelings and emotions or a situation in waking life that terrifies you. Courage will see you through this period of adversity.

Mystical Meaning In the children's poem *Tyger Tyger* by the mystical poet William Blake, the tiger represents material existence. His "fearful symmetry" is the suffering that people experience in the world of opposites, as opposed to innocent oneness with God. Humanity's destiny

TIME

is to regain innocence by passing through the world of experience. Your dream may be dealing with these perplexing cosmic issues.

TIME

Psychological Meaning Preoccupation with time in a dream may reflect your anxieties about being unable to cope with the pressure life imposes on you. Certain times may have specific meanings to you. For example, one minute to midnight implies a pensive situation or a situation that is about to change dramatically. You may associate noontime with lunch and nourishment or five o'clock with finishing work. Perhaps the dream is saying that you must set yourself a deadline or, conversely, set yourself fewer deadlines. And while on the subject of time, did you know that by the time you reach 70 you will have spent about six years of your life dreaming and will have slept for about 20?

Mystical Meaning As you come close to spiritual truth, time becomes less important. Sometimes in dreams, past, present, and future become one. "How are we to know that the mind has become concentrated? Because the idea of time will vanish. The more time passes unnoticed, the more concentrated we are.... All time will have the tendency to come and stand in the one present. So the defini-

tion is given, when the past and present come and stand in one, the mind is said to be concentrated."—Vivekananda

TOILET

Psychological Meaning The cause of your dream may simply be a need to use the toilet. Your unconscious recognizes your body's need and uses the dream to wake you up. Freud had a field day with this one. He associated dreams of excretion with the anal phase of psychosexual development. A child will experience erogenous satisfaction from excretion. A child reprimanded for wetting the bed, or insensitively treated during potty training, may in adult life experience similar feelings of guilt and shame toward sexual functions.

Surprisingly, Freud also believed that a need to use the toilet in dreams represented creativity. Alternatively, dreaming of using the toilet may be a way to show your desire to rid yourself of something that contributes nothing to your well-being, such as an archaic form of behavior or an obsolete lifestyle. Similarly, your unconscious may be drawing your attention to an illness in which using the toilet symbolizes your body's need to rid itself of toxins.

Mystical Meaning Believe it or not, to dream of a toilet indicates legal trouble connected with property deals.

TOMB

Psychological Meaning A tomb may be the entrance to the unconscious. It may also represent those parts of yourself that have been buried away. You may have qualities and talents you are not using. If you dream of seeing your own name above the entrance to the tomb, this is not an omen of death. The dream is saying that what lies within the tomb are the aspects of yourself that have died. You need to rediscover yourself.

Mystical Meaning Your dream may symbolize spiritual death and rebirth. In Celtic times, burial mound tombs were considered to be the womb of the Earth Mother, from which the new spiritual person was born. Later superstitions claim that to dream of a tomb foretells disappointment. Another curious superstition says it foretells a marriage.

TRAVEL

TONGUE

Psychological Meaning A tongue may represent the things you say. You may need to express yourself or may have already said too much. Perhaps you've been saying something "tongue in cheek"? As the tongue plays a part in sexual relations, your dream may be saying something about this area of your life.

Mystical Meaning If you dream of your own tongue, you will tell lies. If you see another person's tongue, they will lie about you. An infected tongue means careless talk.

TOWER

Psychological Meaning A tower may be a symbol for aloofness. Are you so involved in cerebral activities that you have lost touch with your feelings? A tower can also of course be a phallic symbol.

Mystical Meaning To see a tall tower is a sign of good fortune. Climbing a tower brings success, but descending brings failure.

TOY

Psychological Meaning In part, children use toys to develop their social skills and express their role within the family. Dreaming of playing with toys may therefore be an innocuous way to express your hidden feelings. Consider what each toy represents as part of you or your life. Your dream may also be saying that you are only playing with life and must get down to something realistic and practical. The dream could be a pun for toying with ideas or people's feelings.

Mystical Meaning Generally a fortunate omen that predicts happiness for children and families.

TRAFFIC (SEE ALSO CAR)

Psychological Meaning A traffic jam may express your frustration that life is not proceeding as smoothly as you would like it to. You feel stuck. If you dream of being a traffic cop, it may show your desire to impose your own rules on society. You may believe that your social role makes you uncomfortable and alienated from others. Let's face it, not many people like traffic cops.

Mystical Meaning Family problems will be solved but you'll need a lot of patience if the traffic is in a jam, say the wise sages of superstition.

TRAIN (SEE ALSO JOURNEY)

Psychological Meaning Your future is "on track." As trains follow a fixed route, this dream may suggest that you are being helped with your journey through life. To dream of missing a train or passing your destination may indicate that you feel that you have missed an opportunity. Also, are you a conformist? Jung believed that to dream of taking a public vehicle often means that the dreamer is not finding his own way forward and is behaving like everyone else. (Freud believed that to dream of missing a train meant missing death. He also was convinced that all dreams involving motion represented disguised wish fulfillment for sexual intercourse. In particular he claimed that a train represented a penis, and when it went into a tunnel this indicated sexual intercourse.)

Mystical Meaning Dreamers of long ago believed that to dream of traveling indicates a change in fortune. It is particularly fortunate if the destination is toward high hills or mountains. And, if the journey is in a straight line, your good fortune comes swiftly.

TRAPPED

Psychological Meaning This dream probably expresses the way you feel about your situation. You may feel trapped in a marriage, by parenthood, or within a dead-end job. Some areas of your life may need reform. On another level, you may be held captive by your own conservatism or stubbornness. If you change the way you do things, you may gain a greater sense of freedom.

Mystical Meaning The Gypsies say that to dream of seeing an animal trapped in a net indicates that you have to proceed with great caution or your plans will fail.

TRAVEL (SEE JOURNEY)

TREASURE (SEE ALSO MONEY)

I am digging in the garden of my childhood home and have uncovered a box of treasures. My life has been pretty bad lately. Does my dream indicate a change for the better?—P.T., Swindon, England

Psychological Meaning Digging up buried treasure or finding money symbolizes rediscovering a part of yourself. Is there something that you have neglected or repressed? It could be that you had an ambition in life and only now have found the opportunity to try again. There may be a wealth of past experience that you can draw on—something from your childhood, perhaps?

The dream may also have a literal interpretation. If you're worried about finances, now may be the time to start a new venture. The dream may symbolize other things too, such as power, independence, or security. Examine your life; there may be unlooked-for opportunities just below the surface.

ASK YOURSELF

1. *What am I searching for?* The treasure of your dream may symbolize the things you've always wanted from life. They may not necessarily be material, but the dream may suggest that now is the time you are searching your heart to discover what you really want from life.

2. *Is the treasure part of me?* The treasure may symbolize you as a complete and whole person. Maybe something that has hitherto been neglected or repressed is surfacing again. An artistic talent, positive attitude, self-respect, or opportunity, perhaps?

Mystical Meaning Old dream superstitions disagree with the modern interpretations for this dream. To dream of digging for treasure indicates that someone you have loved and trusted is not worthy of your love. However, if you dream of finding gold, in any shape or form, then all will be well.

TREE

Psychological Meaning Trees are symbols of the soul and the life principle. The type and condition of the tree tell of your spiritual condition at the moment. For example, a withered tree may show that you lack inspiration and the desire to live life to the fullest. It may also show your concerns about getting older. Damage to any part of a tree represents damage to aspects of yourself. The tree's branches represent your higher functions; the trunk, your social role; and the roots, the foundations of your personality and unconscious.

Mystical Meaning A tree can also be a symbol of time. The root represent the past; the trunk, the present; and the branches, the future. Perhaps your dream contains a prophecy or says something about your hopes and fears for the future? It is said to be lucky if you dream of climbing a tree.

TRIAL

Psychological Meaning This dream may be your conscience at work. The judge may represent your innermost self. If you are the accused, you may be feeling guilty about something or may be punishing yourself in some way. Who is your accuser? This person may represent an aspect of yourself. Perhaps you are being too hard on yourself?

Mystical Meaning Most dream oracles say that this dream foretells legal disputes.

TRUMPET

Psychological Meaning A loud trumpet may be your unconscious attempting to draw your attention to an issue that you have ignored or are unaware of. The dream may indicate that you should draw attention to yourself or the ideas you have. It may be a pun for "blowing your own horn" or suggesting that you should jazz up your life.

Mystical Meaning To dream of playing a trumpet or hearing one being played is an omen of disappointment, say the oracles.

TWIN

Psychological Meaning Twins represent polarities within the psyche. Examples are introversion and extroversion, ego and shadow, and masculine and feminine. Perhaps the dream is simply saying that you are of two minds about an issue or that you have to duplicate everything you do.

Mystical Meaning Many ancient cultures considered twins to be divine. A very widespread and ancient belief, found among many peoples, says that twins always have different fathers. One of these fathers is supernatural, a god or spirit of some kind. Your dream may be showing you the spiritual side of yourself.

TWO (SEE NUMBERS)

TYRANT (SEE ALSO FATHER)

Psychological Meaning This may be a negative aspect of the father archetype. You may fear being yourself. The dream may also be saying that you are being forced to do something against your will. The tyrant may therefore represent the person or situation that is restricting your personal freedom.

Mystical Meaning Dream oracles interpret this as a contrary dream. You will meet someone nice.

FAMOUS DREAMER

Kirk Douglas
Actor

In 1991, film star Kirk Douglas suffered serious injuries in a helicopter accident after it collided with a light aircraft at Santa Paula, California. He received serious back and head injuries and was fighting for his life. What happened next was more than a dream of flying; Douglas may have really left his body. "It was like I was suspended in space," he said. "There was no concept of time. I saw the most vivid colored lights. It was like a most glorious tunnel of life.

"There was never a moment I was as close to God as I was then. I will never take life, things, or people for granted again. I'm more appreciative of being able to open my eyes in the morning and see those I love close by."(See also Flying.)

UFO

Psychological Meaning Carl Jung believed that UFOs are a symbol, akin to the reappearance of Christ, representing hope in an age of technology. They take on an almost religious dimension as circular mandala symbols representing the higher self. Jung wrote that the worldwide stories of the UFOs are "a symptom of a universally present psychic disposition." The unconscious can manifest itself everywhere and crosses social divides. In dreams, UFOs may represent your desire to find the true spiritual purpose of life and the wholeness of self.

Mystical Meaning Why did the ancient dream seers give no interpretation for this dream? Perhaps the knowledge is hidden away somewhere in the ancient X Files?

UGLY

Psychological Meaning An ugly person appearing in a dream may represent an aspect of yourself that frightens or repulses you. You may have repressed or rejected feelings that may be beneficial to your psychological wholeness.

Mystical Meaning The fairy tale *The Beauty and the Beast* illustrates that you should not judge things by their appearance. Similarly, what may at first appear to be a frightening aspect of your self may in reality mask the true self and its inner beauty.

UMBRELLA

Psychological Meaning An umbrella may be a symbol of protection. As rain can represent the release of emotional tension, an umbrella may illustrate that you are prepared for this outpouring of emotion. It could also represent financial protection and security. In the United Kingdom there's a saying about bank loans: "The manager will only lend you an umbrella when the sun shines." Perhaps your dream contains similar puns.

Mystical Meaning To dream that you have lost an umbrella is fortunate. It predicts a valuable present from a relation. However, if you dream of finding one, you will experience a severe loss in business.

UNDERCLOTHES

Psychological Meaning Underclothes may represent your hidden attitudes and prejudices. If you dream of feeling ashamed at being seen in your underwear, it may indicate an unwillingness to reveal your feelings or to have your attitudes made public. What color is your dream underwear? Red may reveal hidden passions; black, dark thoughts; and yellow, a secret cowardice. If your underwear is dirty or torn it may show that you are not at ease with yourself or feel uncomfortable about your sexuality.

Mystical Meaning Some wise dream oracles say that to dream of being in your underclothes is an omen of stolen pleasures that will rebound with grief.

UNDERGROUND

Psychological Meaning The underground usually symbolizes the unconscious. Things that are uncovered, dug up, or that emerge from the ground represent qualities that are coming from the unconscious. If it is repressed material, these images may be frightening and may appear as zombies, rats, or monsters. If you dream of exploring caves or mines, it may show that you are discovering the innermost recesses of the unconscious.

Mystical Meaning To dream of being in the subway predicts a loss of money.

UNDERWORLD

Psychological Meaning Descent into the underworld may represent death and rebirth. If you dream of an underworld like Hell or Hades, it may symbolize your despair. You may need some help in dealing with your emotional problems.

Mystical Meaning Superstition says that this dream predicts a loss of reputation.

UNDRESSED IN PUBLIC

I dreamed of forgetting to wear my clothes to work. It was highly embarrassing—everybody laughed at me!—T.H., Glasgow, Scotland

Psychological Meaning This is a well-known anxiety dream. Dreams like this are sometimes interpreted as a fear of sexual relationships. Alternatively, they can signify the "naked truth" about yourself. Perhaps, you fear failure or that you will make mistakes and be ridiculed? In your waking life, you need to overcome feelings of vulnerability and need to learn self-confidence. Being partly dressed may symbolize that you are not prepared for what lies ahead. Thoroughly examine your plans and perfect them.

Freud believed that to dream of being naked was an unconscious wish for the free, unclothed periods of early life. Most psychologists consider that dreams of nudity highlight feelings of vulnerability. The dreamer may be conscious of faults and failings.

ASK YOURSELF

1. *How do I feel about my nudity?* Anxiety may symbolize the vulnerability mentioned above, but a feeling of approval may symbolize your pleasure at being free of inhibitions. You may be expressing your openness and honesty.

2. *How do people in my dream react to my nudity?* If they mock you, you may be harboring feelings of guilt and a fear of revealing your feelings. You could have a fear of sexual relationships. Indifference may suggest that something you are concerned about revealing is not really very important. Approval suggests a shedding of inhibitions.

Mystical Meaning Dream oracles say that to dream of undressing means that you will make a grave mistake in your business affairs unless you listen to advice.

UNICORN

Psychological Meaning In mythology, unicorns are either white or multi-colored. They unite the spectrum, showing that the one is the essence of the many. They are the mythical embodiment of the inner realm of the imagination. They may also represent power, gentility, and purity. Your dream may be an expression of inspiration and wonder at the marvels of the inner world.

Mystical Meaning Dream oracles say that this dream means you will have some correspondence in connection with official affairs.

UNIFORM

Psychological Meaning Your dream may be commenting on your conservatism. Are you living your life in an overly regimented manner? Perhaps you are conforming too much. Alternatively, you may feel a need to fit in and be less individualistic.

Mystical Meaning Superstition says that this dream indicates that you will make a journey full of adventure and of special interest to you regarding matrimonial matters.

URINE

Psychological Meaning Urine may represent the feelings you reject. You are trying to cleanse yourself of the things that you consider unworthy. However, dreams of urinating are usually caused by a full bladder and have little symbolic significance

Mystical Meaning Urine has for centuries been regarded as a protection against ghosts and evil spirits. Also it was believed that if a girl urinates in a man's shoes he will fall madly in love with her. Clearly, these concepts are of great significance when interpreting your dream.

FAMOUS DREAMER

Charles Dickens
Novelist

One night, Charles Dickens dreamed he saw a woman in a red shawl with her back toward him. "I am Miss Napier," she said as she spun around. The dream seemed to be nonsense but the next night, after giving a literary reading, some friends came backstage and introduced him to a woman they wanted him to meet. Her name was Miss Napier.

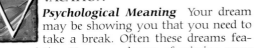

VACATION

Psychological Meaning Your dream may be showing you that you need to take a break. Often these dreams feature anxieties. You may dream of missing your plane, a disaster while on vacation, or a problem such as carrying too much luggage. Listen to what your dream is telling you and take it easy for a while.

Mystical Meaning If a jilted young woman dreams of being on vacation, she will win back the affections of her sweetheart, say the oracles.

VALLEY

Psychological Meaning The mountains on either side of you set limitations on the direction you can go. Your dream may show that the choices you have are limited. You are forced to move forward. A journey through a valley sometimes symbolizes the transition from one set of circumstances to another (i.e., through the valley of death to a new life). You may be going through difficult but ultimately beneficial spiritual changes.

Mystical Meaning As a spiritual dream symbol, a valley may represent judgment and the importance of modesty: "Every valley shall be exalted, and every mountain and hill shall be made low; and the crooked shall be made straight, and the rough places plain" (Isaiah 40:4). Similarly, in the *I Ching* it says: "High mountains are worn down by the waters, and the valleys are filled up. It is the law of fate to undermine what is full and prosper the modest. And men also hate fullness and love the modest."

VAMPIRE (SEE BAT)

VAULT

Psychological Meaning A vault may represent the unconscious. What you find inside may be of significance. For example, if the vault is a crypt, the corpses may represent parts of yourself that are no longer an active part of your personality. They may represent problems and issues that have been laid to rest. If you find yourself in a bank vault, it may symbolize opportunities for happiness and spiritual unfolding. The treasures are your rich psychological potential, which you have found by exploring the unconscious.

Mystical Meaning A very old dream book says: "If a man dreams he is wandering in black vaults or cellars it is a sign he will marry an artful widow and shall be her drudge, never fathoming her wickedness and craft." You can't get more specific than that!

VEGETABLES (SEE ALSO FOOD)

Psychological Meaning These may be a symbol for psychological growth. Your dream may also be telling you that you need to improve your diet.

Mystical Meaning Freud says that dreaming of eating is symbolic of the sexual act and that most vegetables are phallic symbols. He is not alone. Some superstitions claim that vegetables shaped like a man are aphrodisiacs.

VEHICLE (SEE CAR)

VEIL

Psychological Meaning A veil conceals. Are you trying to hide something? Perhaps you are afraid to express part of your personality? Try to decide what is being hidden. A Freudian psychologist interprets a veil as a symbol for a woman's hymen. The dream may show a fear of sexual intercourse.

Mystical Meaning Nuns sometimes wear veils. As a spiritual symbol, this dream could represent a rejection of worldly things. Dream superstition says that to dream of a black veil is a sign of parting from one you love. A white veil indicates a wedding.

VENTRILOQUISM

Psychological Meaning Perhaps you are putting words into people's mouths in waking life. Or maybe you only hear what you want to hear. Projecting your voice may symbolize your desire to influence what people say. Furthermore, ventriloquism can represent a lack of correspondence between your true self and the image you present to the world.

Mystical Meaning Treason is afoot! Be careful in all your dealings, warn the soothsayers.

VICTIM

Psychological Meaning Does your dream amplify feelings that you already have in waking life? You may feel victimized by the people around you. Alternatively, you may have been punishing others, and your dream has turned the tables on you. Your dream may be an expression of your feeling of guilt.

Mystical Meaning According to most dream oracles, this is a dream that should be reversed. You will be victimized if you dream of hurting others, and vice versa if you are the one who is the victim.

VILLAIN

Psychological Meaning A villain may represent part of your personality that needs reform. He may represent the rebellious side of yourself and your secret desire to break the rules of society. Perhaps he represents feelings you have for revenge or your wish to undermine someone's plans. He may represent a vice such as smoking, excessive drinking, or overindulgence.

Mystical Meaning To dream of a ruffian or villain denotes a letter or gift from your sweetheart.

VINE

Psychological Meaning A symbol of plenty. The vine may represent your sensuality and indulgence. Similarly, it may represent the harvest and a time of material prosperity. If your dream deals with health issues, the form of the vine may be suggestive of the nervous system.

Mystical Meaning Any dream connected with vines and grapes is said to be good so long as the vine flourishes. A green vine with green grapes will make your dearest wishes come true.

VIOLENCE

Psychological Meaning If you dream of behaving violently, you may harbor hidden feelings of resentment toward someone who is preventing you from progressing. Alternatively, you may be denying something within yourself. This dream can show the need to assert yourself when dealing with people and to be more accepting of your own failings. You have too much repressed emotion. If the violence in the dream is directed toward you, you may be punishing yourself and you may feel guilty about an issue. Does the outside world make you feel vulnerable at this time? You may feel that everything is against you now, but you should remain hopeful, knowing that a change for the better will inevitably come in time.

Mystical Meaning Another dream that should be reversed, says superstition. If you are violently attacked, it means better times for you.

WATER

VIRGIN

Psychological Meaning Your dream may be nostalgic. Are you looking back to the innocent days before you experienced the pain and complexities of human relationships? A virgin may represent something in your life that is pure and unsullied.

Mystical Meaning The Virgin Mary may represent the anima in a man's dreams. She is a spiritual guide that leads the man to personal wholeness.

VOICES (SEE SOUNDS)

VOLCANO

Psychological Meaning An erupting volcano may be the awakening of negative feelings that have been pushed underground into the unconscious. You may have been holding back your true feelings for so long, you feel that you want to explode.

Mystical Meaning To dream of a volcano is the prelude to a period of peace and happiness. Superstition also says that the happiness is increased if you are nearly enveloped in flames.

VOMIT

Psychological Meaning This dream may be an expression of your desire to be rid of feelings that cause you upset. It may be that you "can't stomach" a situation or feel sick and tired about the way someone has been behaving. In some cases, this dream may represent feelings of self-disgust. For example, you may be so repulsed by something, it makes you want to vomit. You need to quickly get to the heart of these extreme feelings.

Mystical Meaning To dream of vomiting, say the ancient lost texts, shows that the poor shall profit from the rich man's loss.

VULTURE

Psychological Meaning Vultures are horrible creatures who live off the misfortune of other animals. Some people are like this. Are you? Or perhaps someone is taking advantage of you?

Mystical Meaning The Gypsies believe that to dream of vultures indicates that you are surrounded by corrupt people.

 WAGON

Psychological Meaning A wagon may represent slow but sure progress. If you dream of being on a wagon train of pioneers, it may show your desire to explore the unconscious or your hope for a more exciting lifestyle. The dream may be a pun for temperance, "on the wagon."

Mystical Meaning If you ride someone else's wagon you will be poor, but if you dream it is your own you will be rich, says ancient folklore.

WAITER

Psychological Meaning A waiter may represent a helpful influence or a person in your life who is being of service to you. It may also be a pun for "waiting"; your dream may be telling you not to act yet. A waiter does the bidding of others. Perhaps you feel that people treat you like their personal servant?

Mystical Meaning The most reliable superstitions say that if you dream of being served by a waiter at a hotel there will be good luck, but the dream spells trouble if you're served in your own home.

WALL

Psychological Meaning A wall may represent an obstacle that prevents you from attaining what you want. This may be an obstruction from real life or something within yourself. Perhaps you are being like a brick wall by refusing to show your feelings, or perhaps someone you know is. Alternatively, it may represent a problem you cannot solve yet. You've come up against "a brick wall."

Mystical Meaning Walls spell difficulty and obstacles relating to money. But all bodes well if you dream of finding a gateway through.

WAR

Psychological Meaning A war is being waged within yourself. Is it necessary, or would a reconciliation be better than victory? You may feel a conflict between what you want to do and what you think you ought to do. Perhaps you are being too hard on yourself? Carl Jung considered dreams of war to be between the dreamer's conscious and unconscious minds. They may represent the struggle between the deep instinctive forces and the rules of con-

WEDDING

scious conduct. However, sometimes this inner turmoil is necessary in order to allow the wisdom of the conscience to activate. Accept that part of yourself that is trying to find expression. Through acceptance comes peace.

Mystical Meaning A warning of difficulties and danger.

WASHING

Psychological Meaning Washing may represent inner cleansing. You are getting rid of old attitudes, habits, and emotional reactions. If you wash clothes, it may symbolize an improvement in the way you present yourself to the world. Washing plates may indicate purity of psychological nourishment. Washing underwear may indicate the resolution of feelings of sexual uncertainty. Washing another person may show your desire to make that person better.

Mystical Meaning It is auspicious to dream of washing clothes or white linen, but stained clothes predict misfortune. It is also fortunate to dream of washing yourself. However, beware if you dream of taking a bath fully clothed, for this means disappointment.

WATCH (SEE CLOCK)

WATER

Psychological Meaning Water usually represents feelings and emotions. Like the waters of the womb, it can also represent security, life, and birth. The nature of the water can reveal your emotional state. For example, if you dream of crashing waves or rocky seas, it may show that your emotions are out of control. A fast-flowing river may show emotions that are rushing ahead too fast, but if the waters are peaceful, then so are you.

Mystical Meaning Deep pools and lakes of water can represent the unconscious. Like the lake in the King Arthur legends, magical gifts may appear to change your life.

WATERFALL

Psychological Meaning A waterfall may represent exuberance and an uninhibited outpouring of creative energy. You are celebrating life. However, if you dream of being pulled over a waterfall in a boat, your feelings and excitement are out of control and may be getting the better of you. You've gone over the top.

Mystical Meaning There are two traditional interpretations of this dream. You will either be invited to a place of amusement or you will be gossiped about. I suggest you book tickets to Las Vegas.

WEAPONS

Psychological Meaning Weapons can represent anger, resentment, or conflict in your life. If you dream of using weapons against a person you know, it may indicate that you harbor hidden anger or resentment. Perhaps you have not expressed this in waking life. If you do not know the person, then he or she may represent aspects of yourself that you don't like. You may have inner conflicts that need to be resolved. Swords, arrows, knives, guns, and daggers are also phallic symbols showing aggressive male sexuality.

Mystical Meaning The books of dream fortune say that this dream means that you have enemies who pose as friends. Be careful, or they will betray your confidence.

WEATHER

Psychological Meaning The weather in a dream may represent your state of mind. Stormy skies may show arguments and anger; sunshine may show happiness; rain may show release from tension; and snow may indicate that your emotions are frozen.

Mystical Meaning Dreaming of fine weather predicts happy events, but if the weather is bad so are your fortunes.

WEDDING (SEE ALSO RITUALS)

Psychological Meaning A wedding is a union of opposites. To dream of a wedding is most likely to represent the coming together of the opposite aspects of your personality. For example, the couple may represent the fundamental creative forces of life—male and female, matter and spirit, conscious and unconscious, rationality and imagination. This union of diverse forces in your psyche suggests that you will achieve inner wholeness.

Mystical Meaning There are mixed interpretations for this dream in the old dream books. Generally it is seen as a good omen and a possible prophecy for marriage. And here's a horrible superstition that will keep you awake: In many parts of Europe it is believed that whoever falls asleep first on their wedding night will be the first to die.

WEEDS

Psychological Meaning Weeds represent the habits and attitudes that disrupt your inner harmony. Weed out bad habits and you'll be a much better person and feel greater happiness. Your dream is showing you ways to improve yourself. On another level, weeds may represent people in your life who are not contributing to the good of the whole. They may be selfish, stingy, or have a corrupting influence. Root out these bad "friends."

Mystical Meaning To dream of gathering weeds is a good sign. Some sources say that it brings tremendous good luck, but not if the weeds are nettles or thistles, for these predict misfortune.

WEEPING

Psychological Meaning Dreams confront you with emotional issues that you would usually rather avoid in waking life. Clearly, something is upsetting you deeply. The other symbols in the dream may help you identify the cause of your unhappiness.

Mystical Meaning The oracles say that this is a contrary dream denoting festivity, joy, and laughter.

WELL

Psychological Meaning The earth symbolizes the unconscious, and the feelings are symbolized by water. A well is therefore a symbol to show that you can access the deepest recesses of the unconscious. From this source you may draw up into your consciousness emotions, knowledge, happiness, and wisdom. It is the foundation of life, the divine nature.

Mystical Meaning Psychologist Carl Jung was inspired by the imagery of the 5,000-year-old Chinese oracle, the *I Ching*. In the hexagram of *The Well*, it augurs supreme good fortune for this symbol: "It has a spring and never runs dry. Therefore it is a great blessing to the whole land.

The same is true of the really great man, whose inner wealth is inexhaustible; the more that people draw from him, the greater his wealth becomes."

WHEEL (SEE ALSO CIRCLE)

Psychological Meaning The turning of a wheel may represent the progress of your life. If it is broken or there are obstructions, it may symbolize that you feel that things are not working out as you would like. If you dream of being at the wheel of a car, it may show that you have taken control of your progress.

Mystical Meaning Your dream may be an insight into the nature of reality. The Buddha said: "As long as one feels that he is the doer, he cannot escape from the wheel of births."

WHIP

Psychological Meaning Your dream may have sexual undertones in which the whip is a negatively charged symbol of sexual submission. Also, it can represent your awareness of power, domination, and obedience in relationships. The whip may be a symbol of authority or simply may be telling you that you need to whip up your enthusiasm for something.

Mystical Meaning The dream oracles say that if you dream of whipping someone you will soon experience trouble. However, if you dream of being whipped, you will "render a good service to someone."

WHITE (SEE COLORS)

WIFE

Psychological Meaning This dream may be about your real wife or may represent feminine qualities. A Freudian analysis may propose that the way you relate to her may contain elements reminiscent of your relation with your mother.

Mystical Meaning To dream of an unmarried man walking with a woman who claims to be his wife indicates unexpected news.

WIG (SEE ALSO BALDNESS)

Psychological Meaning For a man, this dream may be revealing your feelings of insecurity and a desire to hide your feelings of insufficiency. Are you trying to disguise an aspect of your personality you feel ashamed about? For a woman, dreaming of wigs may symbolize her desire to change the way she presents herself to the world. Are you pretending to be someone you're not?

Mystical Meaning Surprisingly, there are many dream interpretations about wigs. A blond wig means you will have many admirers, a dark wig brings loyalty, a white wig predicts riches, and a brunette wig predicts that the person you marry will be poor.

WILDERNESS

Psychological Meaning This dream may represent a time of self-assessment and a spiritual beginning. Great men like Jesus, the Tibetan lamas, or Hindu sages spent time in the solitary wastelands in order to come closer to their spiritual nature. Away from the distractions of the world, they can recognize the divine within. Your dream expresses the same sentiments.

Mystical Meaning If you dream of walking through a wilderness, this signifies difficulties concerning a cherished plan. If the sun is shining, the final outcome will be successful.

WIND

Psychological Meaning Dreams about wind can symbolize unsettled emotions. You may feel that there's a need for a change in your life.

Mystical Meaning Dreaming of wind predicts troubles ahead. However, it may be comforting to know that this dream predicts that someone else will be made happy by your loss.

WINDOW

Psychological Meaning A window may represent the way you view your circumstances. If you look out a window it may represent your view of the world, but if you are on the outside looking in, then the window represents your view of yourself. Freud considered windows to be feminine sexual symbols.

Mystical Meaning A joyful scene viewed from a window bodes happiness ahead. But if you witness a dreadful event, trouble will affect you. A broken window means disappointment.

WINE

Psychological Meaning Red wine may symbolize blood and therefore the life force. To dream of drinking wine may augur well for health and show that you are starting a more satisfying phase of life. Red wine could also symbolize the passions. Old bottled wine may symbolize maturity.

Mystical Meaning In France, and now in California, it is believed to be bad luck to pass wine around a table in a counterclockwise direction. To dream of drinking wine is a sign of a comfortable home. If wine is spilled, someone will be injured. If you dream of making wine, you will have success. And if you dream about being drunk on wine, you will soon have a big success.

WINNING

Psychological Meaning If you dream of winning a prize or contest, this illustrates your feeling of confidence. It may be a reassurance from your unconscious that you have what it takes to gain success.

Mystical Meaning The dream oracles suggest that this dream means the opposite.

WISE PERSON

Psychological Meaning Listen to the advice given to you by a wise person in your dreams. It is likely to be exactly the guidance you need. It is the unconscious guiding you.

Mystical Meaning Some oracles claim that this dream means you will soon receive a message.

WITCH

Psychological Meaning Since the advent of Christianity, witches have been given bad press. Their original role was as priestesses of the Earth Mother and as bringers of divine wisdom and healing. A witch may represent these qualities in you. In most dreams, witches represent the destructive aspect of the unconscious. This may be the result of repression of a part of yourself that is trying to gain recognition. She may encapsulate negative qualities such as moodiness, dislike of women, deceit, or jealousy. You will need to consider your personal associations with this image and notice the feelings that the dream triggers to fully understand its exact meaning.

Mystical Meaning The fear of the devil and his witches lies at the heart of many omens and superstitions. Since the Middle Ages, it has been believed that dreams of witches are an ill omen.

WOLF

Psychological Meaning Wolves are usually seen as something threatening that attacks during the night, when you are most vulnerable. In dreams they can represent everything you are afraid of in yourself, including self-destructive tendencies, aggression, or uncontrolled sexual desire. They could also represent a worldly trouble, such as a financial problem, i.e., "keeping the wolf from the door." Celtic revivalists give the wolf better press. It is your instinctive nature, your familiar that guides you through the forests of the night

Mystical Meaning The wolf in the story of *Little Red Riding Hood* represents the frightening aspect of the male and the fear of sexual contact. Told at bedtime, the fairy tale warned girls of the dangers of sex before marriage.

WOMAN

Psychological Meaning If you are a woman, a female figure may be a symbol for yourself. She may also symbolize your mother. How you react to her and what she says may reveal a great deal about the way you deal with people in waking life. If you are a man, a woman may represent the other half of your personality—the side of you that is intuitive, sensitive, and nurturing. She may appear in a helpful or fearful guise depending on the degree of acceptance you have for your anima.

Mystical Meaning It is deemed fortunate by superstition to see many women in your dream, for this brings wealth and fame. There are also specifics. An ugly woman means worry, but a beautiful one means happiness; a woman dreaming of being pregnant will have happy news; and if a woman dreams of being a man, she will one day give birth to a son.

WOMB

Psychological Meaning Psychiatrists have suggested that a dream of returning to the womb may represent a deep need for security. It is the ultimate protective love of the mother. Womb symbols may occur in dreams as caves, rooms, or confined yet protected spaces. They are a retreat from life's problems.

Mystical Meaning In the mystical teachings of Kundalini yoga, the "green womb" is a name for Ishvara (Shiva) emerging from his latent condition. This dream may therefore be deeply spiritual, showing awakening higher consciousness.

WORKSHOP

Psychological Meaning You may be undertaking work on yourself. Your dream may give you methods to start this self-improvement. Perhaps the thing being fixed or made gives you a clue about what aspect of yourself needs attention. Your dream may also give solutions to practical problems and show latent skills that you may want to develop.

Mystical Meaning To dream of workers or a workshop is an excellent sign, for according to superstition, this means happiness in both love and business.

WORMS

Psychological Meaning These may be phallic symbols. Associated with dirt and decay, worms may indicate that you have a negative attitude toward sex. Alternatively, they may symbolize helplessness. If you feel downtrodden and oppressed, perhaps its time for the "worm to turn." If you are a gardener, worms may represent something positive. Worms are great in the compost heap and in the garden. They aerate the soil, eat predatory bugs, and just generally do wonderful things. As a dream symbol they may show that you are transforming a bad situation into a good one. For an angler worms may represent bait. Are you "baiting an argument" or perhaps preparing to "fish for compliments"?

Mystical Meaning Dream books claim that worms indicate a danger of infectious diseases. If you dream of destroying worms, you will receive money.

WRAPPING

Psychological Meaning Are you trying to hide something about yourself? Dreaming of wrapping something may be a symbol to show that you conceal your feelings. Unwrapping something may show the opposite—you are beginning to open up. The dream may also be a play on words, to say that you have concluded something—you've "wrapped it up."

Mystical Meaning To dream of receiving a parcel is considered fortunate, but to unwrap it spells bad luck.

WRITING

Psychological Meaning Your dream may be revealing your thoughts and true feelings. The person the writing is addressed to may represent the nature of the issues that you are trying to express. If you dream of someone else writing, it may show an aspect of yourself that is seeking to express itself. The contents of the document may include useful messages from your unconscious.

Mystical Meaning Mystical traditions emphasize the importance of wordless inner silence. "To reconnect consciousness with the unconscious, to make consciousness symbolical is to reconnect words with silence; to let the silence in. If consciousness is all words and no silence, the unconscious remains unconscious."—N. O. Brown

X RAY

Psychological Meaning An X ray may show that you've seen through a problem or issue that has been troubling you. It may refer to the fact that you are perceptive about what motivates people. Perhaps your dream may have identified a health problem of which you are unaware.

Mystical Meaning Sadly, no mystical traditions are associated with X rays, but it is interesting to note that Marie Curie, the discoverer of radium, is said to have been very interested in Spiritualism, mysticism, and dreams.

YELLOW (SEE COLORS)

YOUNG MAN/YOUNG WOMAN
(SEE ANIMA/ANIMUS AND HERO/HEROINE)

YOUTH

Psychological Meaning A youth may represent psychological qualities within yourself that have not as yet grown to maturity. This dream may also be about vitality and sexual desire. Or the dream may simply highlight your concerns about getting older.

Mystical Meaning There will be a reconciliation of family arguments if you dream of seeing a young person. If a mother dreams that her child is young again, she will experience a period of renewed hope and vigor.

ZERO

Psychological Meaning Zero is represented by a circle, which is a symbol for the wholeness of the self. Alternatively, you may feel it expresses your lot in life. You feel you have nothing.

Mystical Meaning Dream lore says that to dream of naught indicates wasted energy. A change of direction is necessary.

ZIPPER

Psychological Meaning This dream may be a sexual innuendo. A broken zipper may symbolize your frustration at not being able to resolve a problem.

Mystical Meaning Yes, there is a mystical meaning to zippers. If you dream of a broken zipper, it means others will dominate you.

ZODIAC

Psychological Meaning If you dream of your own zodiacal sign, it may represent you. However, other signs represent traits and characteristics associated with the given sign. For example, you may be acting like a determined Aries, a stubborn Taurus, or an eccentric Aquarius. If the whole zodiac wheel is represented, it is a mandala that represents the wholeness of the self, the cosmic you.

Mystical Meaning Some dream oraculums claim that you will emigrate if you dream about the signs of the zodiac.

ZOO

Psychological Meaning A zoo is the place where animals are caged and bred. Has your heart become like a zoo? Do you breed animal-like qualities such as anger, jealousy, and hatred? Alternatively, your dream may represent your good psychological qualities that need to be released. You must decide.

Mystical Meaning Zoos predict lots of travel and an enjoyable sojourn in a foreign country. If you dream that a child is with you, there will be great good fortune.

ABOUT THE AUTHOR

Craig Hamilton-Parker is one of the United Kingdom's most famous mediums. Together with his wife, Jane, he has been featured on hundreds of TV programs, and the two have been the resident psychics for one the country's top morning shows. Craig and his wife have interpreted dreams and demonstrated mediumship and clairvoyance to millions of viewers worldwide. Craig Hamilton-Parker also writes articles on the paranormal for national newspapers in England, Scotland, Ireland, South Africa, and Australia. He writes columns about dreams and astrology for many magazines. His website and dream chatroom (http://www.psychics.co.uk) have extensive sections about dreams and more dream experiments.

Index

Famous Dreamers

A

B

C

CLOUDS *See also:* SKY.
CLOVER *See:* FIELDS.
CLOWN *See also:* HERO.
CLUBS *See:* CARDS.
COCK *See:* BIRD.
COCKTAIL *See:* MIXING.
COLORS *See also:* CLOTHES.
CONFLICT *See:* WAR.
CONSTELLATIONS *See:* SKY.
COOKING *See also:* FOOD; OVEN.
COUNTRY HOUSE *See:* HOUSE.
COUPLE *See also:* ANIMA/ANIMUS.
COW *See also:* ANIMALS; MOTHER.
CRAWLING *See:* HOLE.
CRIME *See:* DETECTIVE.
CROCODILE *See also:* ANIMALS.
CROSS *See also:* MANDALA.
CROSSROADS *See also:* ROAD.
CRUISE SHIP *See:* SHIP.
CRYING *See:* EMOTIONS.
CRYPT *See:* VAULT.
CUPBOARD *See also:* CLOTHES; MASK;
  MOTHER.
CURLING IRON *See:* IRON.
CUTTING *See also:* FINGER; HEDGE.

D

DAFFODIL *See also:* COLORS; MANDALA.
DAGGER *See:* KNIFE; WEAPONS.
DARKNESS *See also:* BAT.
DEATH *See also:* FUNERAL; KISS.
DECAY *See:* APPLES; BUILDINGS.
DEN *See:* HOUSE.
DESCENT *See also:* ELEVATOR;
  LADDER; LIFT; TOWER;
  UNDERWORLD.
DESERT *See:* JOURNEY.
DEVIL *See also:* BAT.
DIAMONDS *See:* CARDS; JEWELS.
DIGGING *See:* TREASURE.
DISGUISE *See also:* MASK.
DIVINE CHILD *See:* CHILD.
DOG *See also:* ANIMALS; CHAINS;
  EXCREMENT; LEADING.
DOOR *See also:* OPENING.
DOORKNOB *See:* DOOR.
DOVE *See:* BIRD.
DREAMING OF PAST LIVES *See:* ARMOR.
DRINKING *See:* BLOOD; MILK.
DRIVING *See:* CAR.

E

EAGLE *See:* BIRD.
EARACHE *See:* EAR.
EARLY MIDDLE AGE *See:* SEASONS.
EARTH *See also:* DIRT; ELEMENTS;
  FIELDS; GRAVE; WELL.
EAST *See:* COMPASS; JOURNEY.
EATING *See also:* ANIMALS; FOOD;
  VEGETABLES.
ECLIPSE *See:* MOON.
EGG *See also:* NEST; SHELLS.
EGGSHELL *See:* SHELL.
EIGHT *See:* NUMBERS.
ELEMENTS *See also:* AIR; EARTH; FIRE;
  WATER.
ELEPHANT *See also:* CHAINS.
ELEVATOR *See also:* LIFT.
EMERALDS *See:* JEWELS.
EMOTIONS *See also:* SHADOW.
EMPEROR *See:* FATHER.
EMPTY *See also:* BOTTLE; CUPBOARD;
  PURSE.
ENERGY *See:* ELEMENTS.
ESCAPE *See also:* CHASE.
ETHER *See also:* ELEMENTS.
EVIL EYE *See:* EYES.
EXECUTIONER'S AXE *See:* AXE.
EXPLOSION *See:* BOMB.

F

FACE *See also:* MASK.
FASTING *See:* EATING.
FATHER *See also:* INCEST; MOTHER.
FIGHTING *See also:* ANIMALS; WAR.
FINDING *WAY* *See:* JUNGLE.
FIRE *See also:* ELEMENTS; MADNESS.
FISH *See also:* ANIMALS.
FIST *See:* HAND.
FIVE *See:* NUMBERS.
FLOWER *See also:* MANDALA; ROAD.
FLY *See:* INSECTS.
FLYING *See also:* KIRK DOUGLAS.
FOG *See also:* BLIND; CLOUDS.
FOOD *See also:* BAG; EATING; FEAST;
  KITCHEN.
FOREIGN COUNTRIES *See also:*
  JOURNEY.
FOREST FIRE *See:* FIRE.
FOUNTAIN *See also:* GARDEN;
  MANDALA; WATER.
FOUR *See:* NUMBERS.
FOX *See:* ANIMALS.
FRACTURED LIMBS *See:* BONES.
FROZEN FOOD *See:* FOOD.
FRUIT *See:* FOOD; MARKET.
FUNERAL *See also:* DEATH.

G

GEESE *See:* BIRD.
GENIE *See:* BOTTLE.
GINGER *See:* SMELL.

GLOVES *See:* HAT.
GOLD *See also:* JEWELS; MELTING;
  PURSE; TREASURE.
GORGING ONESELF *See:* EATING.
GRAPES *See:* VINE.
GRAVEN IMAGES *See:* GOD.
GREEN *See:* COLORS; EYES.
GUIDE *See:* SISTER.
GUN *See also:* WEAPONS.

H

HAIR *See also:* MADNESS.
HALL *See also:* BUILDINGS.
HANDS *See also:* NAIL.
HANDSOMENESS *See:* MAN.
HATRED *See:* EVIL.
HAWK *See:* BIRD.
HEARTS *See:* CARDS.
HERO/HEROINE *See also:*
  ANIMA/ANIMUS.
HEXAGRAM *See:* NUMBERS.
HINGES *See:* DOOR.
HOLE *See also:* RABBIT.
HOLIDAY *See:* VACATION.
HORSE *See also:* RIDING.
HOT AIR BALLOON *See:* BALLOON.
HOUSE *See also:* BUILDINGS; EMPTY;
  FIRE; STORM.
HOUSEHOLD IRON *See:* IRON.
HUNT *See also:* CHASE.

I

ICE *See also:* MELTING; WATER.
IMPEDIMENT *See:* DAM.
IRONING *See:* IRON.

J

JAM *See also:* HONEY.
JASMINE *See:* SMELL.
JEALOUSY *See:* EVIL.
JEWELS *See also:* TREASURE.
JOURNEY *See also:* ACCIDENTS;
  AIRPLANE; CAR; HILL; TRAIN.
JUDGE *See also:* TRIAL.
JUNK *See:* BAG.

K

KILLING *See also:* GUN; MONSTER.
KING *See also:* FATHER; QUEEN.
KITCHEN *See also:* BUILDINGS.
KITE *See:* FLYING.
KNIFE *See also:* WEAPONS.

L

L.S.D.   *See:* PILL.
LABORATORY   *See also:* ALCHEMY.
LADDER   *See also:* CLIMBING.
LADYBUG   *See:* INSECTS.
LAKE   *See also:* WATER.
LARD   *See:* EATING.
LATE FOR A TEST   *See:* EXAMINATION.
LATE MIDDLE AGE   *See:* SEASONS.
LAVENDER   *See:* SMELL.
LEMONS   *See:* FOOD.
LETTERS   *See also:* GIFT.
LIBRARY   *See also:* HOUSE.
LIFEBOAT   *See:* SHIP.
LIFT   *See also:* ELEVATOR.
LIGHT   *See also:* LAMP.
LIGHTNESS   *See:* FEATHER.
LION   *See also:* EAGLE; TAMING.
LIQUID   *See:* ELEMENTS.
LIVING ROOM   *See:* HOUSE; ROOMS.
LOCUST   *See:* INSECTS.
LOST   *See also:* CITY; HAT; JUNGLE;
   PURSE.
LOVE   *See:* FAILURE.
LOWER FLOORS   *See:* BUILDINGS.
LUCID DREAMS   *See also:* AWAKENING.
LUNATIC   *See:* MADNESS.
LUSH SCENERY   *See:* JOURNEY.

M

MAGPIE   *See:* BIRD.
MANA PERSONALITIES   *See:* GURU.
MANDALA   *See also:* GARDEN;
   NUMBERS; UFO; ZODIAC.
MARRIAGE   *See:* WEDDING.
MASTER   *See:* BOX.
MEALS   *See:* EATING.
MERMAID   *See also:* ANIMA/ANIMUS;
   SEA.
MESSAGE   *See:* LETTER.
MICE   *See also:* RAT.
MILK   *See:* BOTTLE; FOOD.
MINE   *See:* UNDERGROUND.
MIRROR   *See:* FACE.
MONEY   *See also:* BANK; PURSE; SHOP;
   TREASURE.
MONKEY   *See also:* ANIMALS.
MONSTER   *See also:* CAVE; GIANT;
UNDERGROUND.
MOON   *See also:* LIGHT.
MOSCOW   *See:* JOURNEY.
MOTHER   *See also:* DEATH; FIELDS;
   INCEST.
MOTORBIKE   *See:* RIDING.
MOUNTAIN   *See also:* CLIMBING;
   VALLEY.

MUD   *See:* FALLING.
MUDDLED WORDS   *See:* FAILURE.

N

NAKED   *See also:* NUDITY.
NAKED WOMAN   *See:* CLOTHES.
NET   *See:* TRAPPED.
NETTLES   *See:* WEEDS.
NIGHTMARE   *See:* FEAR.
NINE   *See:* NUMBERS.
NORTH   *See:* COMPASS.
NORTHEAST   *See:* COMPASS.
NORTHWEST   *See:* COMPASS.
NUDITY   *See also:* UNDRESSING.
NUMBERS   *See also:* MANDALA.
NURSING   *See:* BABY.
NUTMEG   *See:* SMELL.

O

OBSTACLE   *See also:* DAM; FENCE;
   STORM; WALL.
OCEAN   *See:* SEA.
OEDIPUS   *See:* MOTHER.
OLD AGE   *See:* SEASONS.
OLD MAN   *See:* AGE; BEARD.
OLD PEOPLE   *See:* AGE.
OLD WOMAN   *See:* AGE.
ONE   *See:* NUMBERS.
OPEN   *See:* CURTAIN; DOOR; GATE;
   JOURNEY.
OPERATION   *See:* HEART.
ORANGE   *See:* COLORS.
ORGY   *See:* PARTY.
OVEN   *See also:* BAKING.
OWL   *See also:* BIRD.
OX   *See:* ANIMALS.

P

PAINTING   *See also:* COLORS.
PALM   *See:* HAND.
PALM TREE   *See:* PARADISE.
PARALYSIS   *See also:* DUMB.
PARIS   *See:* JOURNEY.
PASSING A DESTINATION   *See:* TRAIN.
PAST LIVES   *See:* ARMOR.
PEACHES   *See:* FOOD.
PENTAGRAM   *See:* NUMBERS.
PERSONA   *See:* MASK.
PHALLUS   *See:* FATHER.
PIG   *See also:* ANIMALS.
PILOT   *See:* AIRPLANE.
PIN   *See:* NEEDLE.
PLAGUE   *See:* MICE.
PLANE CRASH   *See:* AIRPLANE.
PLATES   *See:* WASHING.

POINT   *See:* NUMBERS.
POISON   *See:* BOTTLE.
POMEGRANATES   *See:* FOOD.
POOL   *See:* GARDEN; WATER.
POTIONS   *See:* MIXING.
PRIEST   *See also:* ALTAR.
PUBLIC PLACE   *See:* STATION.
PUBLIC SPEAKING   *See:* AUDITION.
PULPIT   *See:* AUDITION.
PUNISHMENT   *See also:* STICK.
PUPIL   *See:* SCHOOL.
PURPLE   *See:* COLORS.

Q

QUARRY   *See also:* CHASE.
QUEEN   *See also:* ANIMA/ANIMUS;
   KING; MOTHER.

R

RAILROAD   *See:* TRAIN.
RAIN   *See also:* UMBRELLA; WEATHER.
RAINBOW   *See also:* LIGHT.
RAM   *See:* SHEEP.
RASH   *See:* SKIN.
RAT   *See also:* BAT; MICE;
   UNDERGROUND.
RED   *See:* BOTTLE; COLORS; PAINTING;
   SKY; UNDERCLOTHES.
RED WINE   *See:* BOTTLE.
REJECTION   *See also:* ABANDONMENT.
RELATIONSHIP   *See also:* TABLE.
REVENGE   *See:* EVIL.
RIVER   *See also:* WATER.
ROAD   *See also:* JOURNEY.
ROBOT   *See:* MASK.
ROCKY PATH   *See:* JOURNEY.
ROCKY ROAD   *See:* PATH.
ROOF   *See:* HOUSE.
ROOMS   *See also:* BUILDINGS; EMPTY;
   WOMB.
ROOTS   *See:* TREE.
ROSE   *See also:* MANDALA.
RUBBISH   *See:* GARBAGE.
RUBIES   *See:* JEWELS.
RULES   *See:* POLICE.

S

SAILING   *See:* ROCK; SEA.
SAILOR   *See also:* ROCK.
SALT   *See:* EATING.
SAPPHIRES   *See:* JEWELS.
SATHYA SAI BABA (SUTRA VAHINI)   *See:*
   BRIDGE; GURU; HEART; LUGGAGE;
   MONKEY; PLAY; STRUGGLE.
SAVAGE   *See also:* SHADOW.
SCARAB   *See:* INSECTS.

SCARECROW *See:* MASK.
SCHOOL *See also:* EXAMINATIONS.
SCHOOLTEACHER *See:* SCHOOL.
SCISSORS *See also:* CUTTING.
SCOLDING *See:* SCHOOL.
SCULPTOR *See:* STATUE.
SEA *See also:* DIVING; DOLPHIN; FISH;
    ISLAND; RESCUE; SHIP; WATER.
SEVEN *See:* NUMBERS.
SEWING *See:* NEEDLE; REPAIRING.
SHADOW SELF *See:* FRIEND.
SHAPES *See:* MANDALA; NUMBERS.
SHARK *See:* BITE.
SHEEP *See also:* LAMB.
SHEPHERD *See:* SHEEP.
SHIP *See also:* SAILOR.
SHIPWRECK *See:* SHIP.
SHOT *See:* GUN.
SHRIVELED *See:* ABDOMEN; BREASTS.
SIGNPOST *See also:* CITY; CROSSROADS.
SILVER *See also:* MELTING.
SINKING *See also:* DROWNING.
SISTER *See also:* ANIMA/ANIMUS;
    SHADOW.
SIX *See:* NUMBERS.
SKELETON *See:* BONES.
SKULL *See also:* BONES.
SKY *See also:* FLYING.
SLEEP PARALYSIS *See:* DUMB.
SNAKES *See also:* ANIMALS; EAGLE.
SNOW *See also:* ICE; WEATHER.
SOIL *See:* DIRT.
SOLID *See:* ELEMENTS.
SONG *See:* MUSIC.
SOUNDS *See also:* FLYING; MUSIC.
SOUTH *See:* COMPASS.
SOUTHEAST *See:* COMPASS.
SOUTHWEST *See:* COMPASS.
SPADES *See:* CARDS.
SPIRITS *See:* GHOST.
SPRING *See:* SEASONS.
SQUARE *See:* MANDALA; NUMBERS.
STAGE *See:* AUDITION; BACK;
    THEATER.
STARVATION *See:* EATING.
STATION *See also:* JOURNEY; TRAIN.
STORK *See:* BIRD.
STORM *See also:* SHIP; THUNDER;
    WEATHER.
STORY *See also:* BUILDINGS; HOUSE.
STRANGER *See also:* ANGER; SHADOW.
STRAW HAT *See:* HAT.
STREET *See:* ROADS.
SUBMARINE *See:* SHIP.
SUBWAY *See:* UNDERGROUND.
SUFFOCATION *See also:* DROWNING.
SUGAR *See:* FOOD.
SUIT *See also:* CLOTHES.

SUMMER *See:* SEASONS.
SUN *See also:* DAWN; FATHER; LIGHT;
    MANDALA; MOON;
    RAINBOW; WILDERNESS.
SUNRISE *See:* SUN.
SUNSET *See:* SUN.
SUNSHINE *See:* WEATHER.
SWEEPING *See:* BRUSH.
SWOLLEN *See:* ABDOMEN; FACE.
SWORD *See also:* WEAPONS.

T

TEACHER *See:* SCHOOL.
TEACHING *See:* SCHOOL.
TELEVISION *See also:* FILM.
TEMPLE *See:* CHURCH.
TEN *See:* NUMBERS.
TEST *See:* EXAMINATION; FAILURE.
THEATER *See also:* CURTAIN.
THISTLES *See:* WEEDS.
THREE *See:* NUMBERS.
TICKET *See also:* KEY.
TIGER *See also:* ANIMALS.
TOMB *See also:* DESCENT.
TOP FLOOR *See:* STORY.
TOP HAT *See:* HAT.
TORTOISE SHELL *See:* SHELL.
TOWN *See:* CITY; JOURNEY.
TRAFFIC *See also:* CARS.
TRAIN *See also:* FAILURE;
    FRUSTRATION; JOURNEY.
TRAPDOOR *See:* DOOR.
TRAVEL *See:* JOURNEY; TRAIN.
TREASURE *See also:* ANIMALS; DIVING;
    DRAGON; MONEY.
TREE *See also:* AXE; ROAD.
TRIANGLE *See:* MANDALA; NUMBERS.
TRUNK *See:* TREE.
TURKEY *See:* BIRD.
TWO *See:* NUMBERS.

U

UGLINESS *See:* MAN.
UGLY *See also:* WOMAN.
UNDERCLOTHES *See also:* WASHING.
UNDERWEAR *See:* NUDITY.
UNPREPARED *See:* EXAMINATION.
UPSTAIRS *See:* BUILDINGS.

V

VAMPIRE *See:* BAT.
VAPOR *See:* ELEMENTS.
VAULT *See also:* BANK.
VEGETABLES *See also:* FOOD; MARKET.
VEHICLE *See:* CAR.

VESSEL *See:* EMPTY.
VOICES *See:* SOUNDS.

W

WAGON TRAIN *See:* WAGON.
WALKING *See:* WILDERNESS.
WALL *See also:* CITY; CLIMBING.
WARSHIP *See:* SHIP.
WASHING *See also:* BATH; FOOT.
WASP *See:* INSECTS.
WATCH *See:* CLOCK.
WATER *See also:* ANCHOR; BAPTISM;
    BATH; BOAT; DIVING; DROWNING;
    ELEMENTS; FLOATING; FLOOD;
    GARDEN; LAKE; MOON; SWIMMING;
    WELL.
WAVES *See:* WATER.
WEAPON *See also:* FATHER.
WEDDING *See also:* RITUALS.
WEEDS *See:* FIELDS.
WELL *See:* DESCENT.
WEST *See:* COMPASS; JOURNEY.
WHEEL *See also:* CIRCLE.
WHISTLE *See:* SOUNDS.
WHITE *See:* CLOUDS; COLORS; VEIL.
WIG *See also:* BALDNESS.
WIND *See:* AIR.
WINDOWS *See:* HOUSE.
WINE *See also:* BOTTLE; CELLAR; CUP.
WINGS *See:* ANGEL.
WINTER *See:* SEASONS.
WISE OLD MAN *See:* FATHER.
WOMAN WEARING MAN'S HAT *See:* HAT.
WOMB *See also:* BATH; CAVE.
WORKER *See:* WORKSHOP.

Y

YELLOW *See:* COLORS; DAFFODIL;
    UNDERCLOTHES.
YOUNG MAN/YOUNG WOMAN *See:*
    ANIMA/ANIMUS; HERO/HEROINE.
YOUTH *See also:* SEASONS.

Z

ZERO *See also:* NUMBERS.
ZODIAC *See also:* SKY.
ZOMBIES *See:* UNDERGROUND.